W9-BRI-842

IMMIGRATION FROM THE FORMER YUGOSLAVIA

Nancy Honovich

THE CHANGING Face of North America:
IMMIGRATION SINCE 1965

IMMIGRATION FROM THE FORMER YUGOSLAVIA

Nancy Honovich

MASON CREST PUBLISHERS
PHILADELPHIA

Produced by OTTN Publishing, Stockton, New Jersey

Mason Crest Publishers
370 Reed Road
Broomall, PA 19008
www.masoncrest.com

First printing

1 3 5 7 9 8 6 4 2

Library of Congress Cataloging-in-Publication Data

Honovich, Nancy.
  Immigration from the former Yugoslavia : Slovenia, Croatia, Bosnia and Herzegovina, Macedonia, Serbia, and Montenegro /
Nancy Honovich.
    p. cm. — (The changing face of North America)
Summary: An overview of immigration from the six countries that made up Yugoslavia to the United States and Canada since
the 1960s, when immigration laws were changed to permit greater numbers of people to enter these countries.
Includes bibliographical references and index.
  ISBN 1-59084-690-7
  1. Yugoslav Americans—History—20th century—Juvenile literature. 2. Yugoslavs—Canada—History—20th century—
Juvenile literature. 3. Immigrants—United States—History—20th century—Juvenile literature. 4. Immigrants—
Canada—History—20th century—Juvenile literature. 5. Yugoslavia—Emigration and immigration—History—20th
century—Juvenile literature. 6. United States—Emigration and immigration—History—20th century—Juvenile literature.
7. Canada—Emigration and immigration—History—20th century—Juvenile literature. [1. Yugoslav Americans—
History—20th century. 2. Yugoslavs—Canada—History—20th century. 3. Immigrants—United States—History—20th
century. 4. Immigrants—Canada—History—20th century. 5. Yugoslavia—Emigration and immigration—History—20th
century. 6. United States—Emigration and immigration—History—20th century. 7. Canada—Emigration and immigration—History—20th century.] I. Title. II. Series.
  E184.Y7H66 2004
  304.8'730497--dc22
                                                                                                2003016368

THE **CHANGING**
Face of North America:
IMMIGRATION SINCE 1965

CONTENTS

INTRODUCTION

THE CHANGING FACE OF AMERICA

By Senator Edward M. Kennedy

America is proud of its heritage and history as a nation of immigrants, and my own family is an example. All eight of my great-grandparents were immigrants who left Ireland a century and a half ago, when that land was devastated by the massive famine caused by the potato blight. When I was a young boy, my grandfather used to take me down to the docks in Boston and regale me with stories about the Great Famine and the waves of Irish immigrants who came to America seeking a better life. He talked of how the Irish left their marks in Boston and across the nation, enduring many hardships and harsh discrimination, but also building the railroads, digging the canals, settling the West, and filling the factories of a growing America. According to one well-known saying of the time, "under every railroad tie, an Irishman is buried."

America was the promised land for them, as it has been for so many other immigrants who have found shelter, hope, opportunity, and freedom. Immigrants have always been an indispensable part of our nation. They have contributed immensely to our communities, created new jobs and whole new industries, served in our armed forces, and helped make America the continuing land of promise that it is today.

The inspiring poem by Emma Lazarus, inscribed on the pedestal of the Statue of Liberty in New York Harbor, is America's welcome to all immigrants:

Give me your tired, your poor,
Your huddled masses yearning to breathe free,
The wretched refuse of your teeming shore,
Send these, the homeless, tempest-tossed, to me:
I lift my lamp beside the golden door.

The period since September 11, 2001, has been particularly challenging for immigrants. Since the horrifying terrorist attacks, there has been a resurgence of anti-immigrant attitudes and behavior. We all agree that our borders must be safe and secure. Yet, at the same time, we must safeguard the entry of the millions of persons who come to the United States legally each year as immigrants, visitors, scholars, students, and workers. The "golden door" must stay open. We must recognize that immigration is not the problem—terrorism is. We must identify and isolate the terrorists, and not isolate America.

One of my most important responsibilities in the Senate is the preservation of basic rights and basic fairness in the application of our immigration laws, so that new generations of immigrants in our own time and for all time will have the same opportunity that my great-grandparents had when they arrived in America.

Immigration is beneficial for the United States and for countries throughout the world. It is no coincidence that two hundred years ago, our nations' founders chose *E Pluribus Unum*—"out of many, one"—as America's motto. These words, chosen by Benjamin Franklin, John Adams, and Thomas Jefferson, refer to the ideal that separate colonies can be transformed into one united nation. Today, this ideal has come to apply to individuals as well. Our diversity is our strength. We are a nation of immigrants, and we always will be.

FOREWORD

THE CHANGING FACE OF THE UNITED STATES

Marian L. Smith, historian
U.S. Immigration and Naturalization Service

Americans commonly assume that immigration today is very different than immigration of the past. The immigrants themselves appear to be unlike immigrants of earlier eras. Their language, their dress, their food, and their ways seem strange. At times people fear too many of these new immigrants will destroy the America they know. But has anything really changed? Do new immigrants have any different effect on America than old immigrants a century ago? Is the American fear of too much immigration a new development? Do immigrants really change America more than America changes the immigrants? The very subject of immigration raises many questions.

In the United States, immigration is more than a chapter in a history book. It is a continuous thread that links the present moment to the first settlers on North American shores. From the first colonists' arrival until today, immigrants have been met by Americans who both welcomed and feared them. Immigrant contributions were always welcome—on the farm, in the fields, and in the factories. Welcoming the poor, the persecuted, and the "huddled masses" became an American principle. Beginning with the original Pilgrims' flight from religious persecution in the 1600s, through the Irish migration to escape starvation in the 1800s, to the relocation of Central Americans seeking refuge from civil wars in the 1980s and 1990s, the United States has considered itself a haven for the destitute and the oppressed.

But there was also concern that immigrants would not adopt American ways, habits, or language. Too many immigrants might overwhelm America. If so, the dream of the Founding Fathers for United States government and society would be destroyed. For this reason, throughout American history some have argued that limiting or ending immigration is our patriotic duty. Benjamin Franklin feared there were so many German immigrants in Pennsylvania the Colonial Legislature would begin speaking German. "Progressive" leaders of the early 1900s feared that immigrants who could not read and understand the English language were not only exploited by "big business," but also served as the foundation for "machine politics" that undermined the U.S. Constitution. This theme continues today, usually voiced by those who bear no malice toward immigrants but who want to preserve American ideals.

Have immigrants changed? In colonial days, when most colonists were of English descent, they considered Germans, Swiss, and French immigrants as different. They were not "one of us" because they spoke a different language. Generations later, Americans of German or French descent viewed Polish, Italian, and Russian immigrants as strange. They were not "like us" because they had a different religion, or because they did not come from a tradition of constitutional government. Recently, Americans of Polish or Italian descent have seen Nicaraguan, Pakistani, or Vietnamese immigrants as too different to be included. It has long been said of American immigration that the latest ones to arrive usually want to close the door behind them.

It is important to remember that fear of individual immigrant groups seldom lasted, and always lessened. Benjamin Franklin's anxiety over German immigrants disappeared after those immigrants' sons and daughters helped the nation gain independence in the Revolutionary War. The Irish of the mid-1800s were among the most hated immigrants, but today we all wear green on St. Patrick's Day. While a century ago it was feared that Italian and other Catholic immigrants would vote as directed by the Pope, today that controversy is only a vague memory. Unfortunately, some ethnic groups continue their efforts to earn acceptance. The African

Americans' struggle continues, and some Asian Americans, whose families have been in America for generations, are the victims of current anti-immigrant sentiment.

Time changes both immigrants and America. Each wave of new immigrants, with their strange language and habits, eventually grows old and passes away. Their American-born children speak English. The immigrants' grandchildren are completely American. The strange foods of their ancestors—spaghetti, baklava, hummus, or tofu—become common in any American restaurant or grocery store. Much of what the immigrants brought to these shores is lost, principally their language. And what is gained becomes as American as St. Patrick's Day, Hanukkah, or Cinco de Mayo, and we forget that it was once something foreign.

Recent immigrants are all around us. They come from every corner of the earth to join in the American Dream. They will continue to help make the American Dream a reality, just as all the immigrants who came before them have done.

FOREWORD

THE CHANGING FACE OF CANADA

Peter A. Hammerschmidt
First Secretary, Permanent Mission of Canada to the United Nations

Throughout Canada's history, immigration has shaped and defined the very character of Canadian society. The migration of peoples from every part of the world into Canada has profoundly changed the way we look, speak, eat, and live. Through close and distant relatives who left their lands in search of a better life, all Canadians have links to immigrant pasts. We are a nation built by and of immigrants.

Two parallel forces have shaped the history of Canadian immigration. The enormous diversity of Canada's immigrant population is the most obvious. In the beginning came the enterprising settlers of the "New World," the French and English colonists. Soon after came the Scottish, Irish, and Northern and Central European farmers of the 1700s and 1800s. As the country expanded westward during the mid-1800s, migrant workers began arriving from China, Japan, and other Asian countries. And the turbulent twentieth century brought an even greater variety of immigrants to Canada, from the Caribbean, Africa, India, and Southeast Asia.

So while English- and French-Canadians are the largest ethnic groups in the country today, neither group alone represents a majority of the population. A large and vibrant multicultural mix makes up the rest, particularly in Canada's major cities. Toronto, Vancouver, and Montreal alone are home to people from over 200 ethnic groups!

Less obvious but equally important in the evolution of Canadian immigration has been hope. The promise of a better life lured Europeans and Americans seeking cheap (sometimes even free) farmland. Thousands of Scots and Irish arrived to escape grinding poverty and starvation. Others came for freedom, to escape religious and political persecution. Canada has long been a haven to the world's dispossessed and disenfranchised—Dutch and German farmers cast out for their religious beliefs, black slaves fleeing the United States, and political refugees of despotic regimes in Europe, Africa, Asia, and South America.

The two forces of diversity and hope, so central to Canada's past, also shaped the modern era of Canadian immigration. Following the Second World War, Canada drew heavily on these influences to forge trailblazing immigration initiatives.

The catalyst for change was the adoption of the Canadian Bill of Rights in 1960. Recognizing its growing diversity and Canadians' changing attitudes towards racism, the government passed a federal statute barring discrimination on the grounds of race, national origin, color, religion, or sex. Effectively rejecting the discriminatory elements in Canadian immigration policy, the Bill of Rights forced the introduction of a new policy in 1962. The focus of immigration abruptly switched from national origin to the individual's potential contribution to Canadian society. The door to Canada was now open to every corner of the world.

Welcoming those seeking new hopes in a new land has also been a feature of Canadian immigration in the modern era. The focus on economic immigration has increased along with Canada's steadily growing economy, but political immigration has also been encouraged. Since 1945, Canada has admitted tens of thousands of displaced persons, including Jewish Holocaust survivors, victims of Soviet crackdowns in Hungary and Czechoslovakia, and refugees from political upheaval in Uganda, Chile, and Vietnam.

Prior to 1978, however, these political refugees were admitted as an exception to normal immigration procedures. That year, Canada revamped its refugee policy with a new Immigration Act that explicitly affirmed Canada's commitment to the resettlement of refugees from oppression. Today, the admission of refugees remains a central part of Canadian immigration law and regulations.

Amendments to economic and political immigration policy continued during the 1980s and 1990s, refining further the bold steps taken during the modern era. Together, these initiatives have turned Canada into one of the world's few truly multicultural states.

Unlike the process of assimilation into a "melting pot" of cultures, immigrants to Canada are more likely to retain their cultural identity, beliefs, and practices. This is the source of some of Canada's greatest strengths as a society. And as a truly multicultural nation, diversity is not seen as a threat to Canadian identity. Quite the contrary—diversity *is* Canadian identity.

1

LAND OF THE SOUTH SLAVS

Southeastern Europe's Balkan Peninsula, which extends into the Mediterranean Sea east of Italy, is home to 10 nations, including Albania, Bulgaria, Greece, Romania, and a small part of Turkey. It is a rugged, largely mountainous region—in fact, the term *Balkan* comes from a Turkish word meaning "mountain."

The area has also given the English language a word that aptly describes how the peninsula's newest independent countries came into being: *balkanization*, "the breaking up of a region or group into smaller and often hostile units." Beginning in the early 1990s, the Balkan country known as Yugoslavia—which had been created some seven decades earlier in the aftermath of World War I—was torn apart in a series of bloody conflicts fanned by ethnic and religious hatred, historical grievances, and political ambitions. In short order four Yugoslav republics—Slovenia, Croatia, Bosnia and Herzegovina, and Macedonia—declared their independence, and in 2003 the remaining republics, Serbia and Montenegro, decided to reorganize politically as a loose confederation, essentially marking the end of Yugoslavia.

The terrible violence that ripped through Yugoslavia in the late 20th century displaced several million people. Tens of thousands settled in the United States and Canada. But these refugees were by no means the first immigrants from the region to make their way to North American shores. In the

◀ A view of Kranj, a town in northern Slovenia. The smallest and most prosperous of the former Yugoslav republics, Slovenia was also the first to break away.

A planeload of refugees from the Kosovo region of Yugoslavia disembarks in Delaware to begin a new life in the United States.

19th century, long before the country of Yugoslavia even existed, significant numbers of immigrants from the region sailed to North America to start a new life. Today the descendants of these immigrants, along with the more recent arrivals, number more than a million.

Ethnic Identities

One notable characteristic of immigrants from the former Yugoslavia is that they retain a strong sense of ethnic identity. The six republics that made up Yugoslavia contained more than a dozen distinct ethnic groups, the largest and most important of which were the Serbs (or Serbians), Montenegrins, Croats (or Croatians), Slovenes, Bosnian Muslims (or Bosniacs), and Macedonians. These six groups share descent from the Slavs—a collection of peoples spread widely throughout eastern and southeastern Europe—but each group had its own unique beliefs, traditions, customs, and histories. The creation of Yugoslavia—"Land of the South Slavs"—in 1918, and increasing intermarriage during the 20th century, failed to erase these ethnic differences.

The various groups that made up Yugoslavia are, as a rule, extremely proud of their cultural heritage. In North America, that pride finds expression in a number of patriotic, educational, and cultural organizations, which keep alive and celebrate the rich traditions of the different ethnic groups.

Unfortunately, ethnic pride has had a darker side in Yugoslavia. Leaders such as Slobodan Milosevic of Serbia and Franjo Tudjman of Croatia were able to exploit old fears and animosities, pitting one group against another for political gain. In the process, they helped unleash the horrific violence that ultimately destroyed Yugoslavia.

2 A History of Strife

During the Middle Ages, several Croatian, Serbian, and Bosnian kingdoms emerged at the edges of more powerful empires. By the mid-14th century, the largest of these, the kingdom of Serbia, controlled much of the Balkan Peninsula, including modern-day Albania, Macedonia, Montenegro, and parts of eastern Bosnia and Herzegovina and northern Greece.

Soon, however, the Turkish Ottoman Empire began expanding into the Balkans. On June 28, 1389, the Ottomans under Sultan Murad I met a Serb-led force commanded by Prince Lazar at Kosovo Polje ("the Field of Blackbirds"), near present-day Pristina. Both sides suffered heavy casualties.

Militarily, the Battle of Kosovo—which claimed the lives of both Murad and Lazar—was probably not as decisive as some sources suggest; before the battle the Turks had already made significant inroads into Serb territory, and it would take an additional seven decades before the Ottoman conquest of Bosnia was complete and nearly a century before Herzegovina fell. But for Serbs, their defeat at the Battle of Kosovo took on mythic significance. Lazar and his comrades came to be seen not simply as national heroes who died in defense of Serb civilization, but also as martyrs to the Christian faith, which was under attack by the Muslim Turks. And the Eastern Orthodox Serbs believed that Roman Catholic Europe had abandoned them to face the "infidels" alone. Six hundred years later, the

◀Anguish at a refugee camp for Bosnian Serbs, 1995. Yugoslavia's civil wars of the 1990s displaced millions of people, claimed tens of thousands of lives, and ultimately tore the country apart.

Battle of Kosovo would be invoked—to great effect—to stir Serb nationalism.

The Ottoman and Austro-Hungarian Eras

The Ottomans, whose rule in the Balkans lasted into the 20th century, were relatively tolerant, permitting conquered peoples to practice their own religion. Still, there were incentives to convert to Islam: non-Muslims had to pay a special tax, and they could not vote or serve in the government. While the Serbs retained their Eastern Orthodox beliefs and Croats stayed predominantly Roman Catholic, over the years large numbers of ethnic Albanians and Bosnians converted to Islam, further separating the peoples of the region.

By the 19th century, the power of the Ottoman Empire had been declining for about 200 years. In the Balkans, internal revolts and external military pressure, particularly from Russia and the Austro-Hungarian Empire, combined to loosen the Ottomans' grip. In the 1860s Austria-Hungary added Croatia to its territory. (The much smaller Slovenia had been claimed by Austria's Hapsburg monarchy since the 14th century.) In 1878 the Treaty of Berlin, which ended a war between the Russians and the Turks, gave Austria-Hungary control over Bosnia and Herzegovina and recognized the independent states of Serbia and Montenegro (though in reality Russian and Austro-Hungarian influence there was significant). Throughout the Balkans, nationalism simmered, and Austria-Hungary's annexation of Bosnia and Herzegovina in 1908 only made the situation more volatile.

The Balkan Wars and World War I

In 1912 Montenegro, Serbia, Bulgaria, and Greece—encouraged by Russia—joined forces in a war against the Ottoman Empire. The Balkan allies quickly triumphed, pushing the Ottomans out of Kosovo, Macedonia, and Albania. The following year, however, another war broke out over the issue of

This photograph, taken on June 28, 1914, shows Archduke Franz Ferdinand and his wife, Sophie, about an hour before Bosnian Serb nationalist Gavrilo Princip killed them in Sarajevo. The assassination of the heir to the Austrian throne would touch off World War I and forever alter the political landscape of the Balkans.

how to divide up Macedonia. The Second Balkan War pitted Bulgaria against its former allies Greece and Serbia, which were joined by Romania. Bulgaria was defeated, and in the end Serbia controlled Macedonia and Kosovo. Still, some Serb nationalists believed that Serbian territory should also include Bosnia and Herzegovina.

On June 28, 1914—the anniversary of the Battle of Kosovo—Serb nationalists carried out a plot to assassinate Archduke Franz Ferdinand, heir to the Austrian throne, in Sarajevo, Bosnia. The Serbian government ignored Austria-Hungary's demands that it condemn the assassination, arrest people involved in the plot, and suppress nationalism in Bosnia and Herzegovina. Strategic considerations and complex alliances soon drew the great powers of Europe—including Germany, Russia, Great Britain, and France—into the dispute. The result was World War I, the most destructive conflict to that point in history, which the United States joined in 1917.

By war's end in 1918, Austria-Hungary, along with its allies the Ottoman Empire and Germany, had been soundly defeated. In the Balkans this created opportunities for those who wished to incorporate Bosnia and Herzegovina into a larger state.

From the Formation
of Yugoslavia to World War II

In the aftermath of the war, the Kingdom of Serbs, Croats, and Slovenes (later to be renamed Yugoslavia) was created. Almost from the start, however, ethnic and religious divisions plagued the new country. Although a constitutional monarchy with a parliament was established, the king came from a Serb ruling house and Serbs dominated the government. Croats, in particular, believed they were discriminated against, but their fellow Roman Catholic Slovenes and the Bosnian Muslims also became disenchanted with the Orthodox Serbs and their government.

In 1929, in the face of increasing nationalism among the ethnic groups, King Alexander I changed his country's name to Yugoslavia and took the occasion to dissolve the parliament, abolish the constitution, and assume absolute power. This did

Ustasha soldiers stand over the bodies of several people they have shot, 1945. During World War II, Croatia's Ustasha government, a puppet regime of Nazi Germany, persecuted the Serbs.

little to quell unrest, and in 1931 a Croat separatist assassinated the king. Alexander's young son, Peter II, was heir to the throne, but a cousin, Prince Paul, was designated to rule until he reached adulthood.

World War II (1939–1945) unleashed terrible political and ethnic violence in Yugoslavia. After Prince Paul aligned his country with Nazi Germany, he was overthrown in a popular uprising, and Peter II took over. This enraged Germany's leader, Adolf Hitler, who ordered an invasion. The April 1941 German invasion forced Peter to flee to England, where he set up a government in exile. Yugoslavia was divided between Germany and its Italian, Bulgarian, and Hungarian allies. In Croatia and Bosnia, a Croatian Fascist group known as the Ustasha ruled as a puppet government of Nazi Germany. The Ustasha, which wanted to create a "pure" Croatian state, persecuted Serbs, as well as Jews and Gypsies. It carried out countless massacres and set up concentration camps, killing perhaps hundreds of thousands of Serbs. Meanwhile, bands of Serb guerrilla fighters called Chetniks—whose ultimate aim was to restore the Yugoslav monarchy—battled the Ustasha and the German occupying army. They also fought bitterly with other guerrillas who were battling the Germans and the Ustasha—the partisans of Josip Broz Tito, who were predominantly Communists and did not support Peter II's cause. Frequent atrocities and reprisals were committed by all sides.

The Rise of Tito

By the end of World War II, Tito had become the most powerful leader in Yugoslavia. In 1945 he consolidated his authority by outlawing the monarchy and holding elections in which only members of his Communist-dominated party were allowed to run. Yugoslavia was officially proclaimed a federal republic, though in fact the country would remain a Communist dictatorship under Tito for the next 35 years.

The son of a Slovene mother and a Croat father, Tito understood that if Yugoslavia were to hold together, the nationalist aspirations of its various groups would have to be kept in check. The establishment of six supposedly equal republics— Serbia, Croatia, Montenegro, Slovenia, Bosnia and Herzegovina, and Macedonia—and the toleration of limited cultural expression by the peoples of these republics would, it was hoped, provide a manageable outlet for ethnic affiliations. Moreover, Tito took steps to prevent old grievances from reigniting ethnic violence (for example, by forbidding the discussion of the Ustasha's wartime persecution of Serbs).

But not all his methods were so benign, and his goals went beyond reconciling former enemies. "Power," Noel Malcolm wrote in his book *Bosnia, A Short History*, "was more important to Tito than reconciliation, and Communist power was imposed on Yugoslavia at a very heavy price. . . . Altogether it has been estimated that up to 250,000 people were killed by Tito's mass shootings, forced death marches and concentration camps in the period 1945–6." Among the victims were Serb Chetniks and opponents of communism.

Tito's Yugoslavia displayed many characteristics of Soviet-style communism. In the economic realm, the government took control of all industry, allocating resources and imposing unrealistic five-year plans for the rapid increase of industrial production. Politically, only the Communist Party was legal, expressions of dissent were met with intimidation or imprisonment, and intellectual freedom of all types was restricted. Social control was maintained through an extensive secret police apparatus.

At the same time, Yugoslavian communism differed in several significant respects from the Soviet version. For example, Tito never collectivized agriculture, instead permitting small farmers to continue growing crops on their own land (though a portion had to be given to the government). And Yugoslavia, unlike most of Eastern Europe, avoided falling under Soviet domination. By charting an independent course, Tito was able to reap some of the benefits of economic ties with the industrialized West. (Western Europe and the United States were aligned

Josip Broz Tito greets a crowd of well-wishers from his train, circa 1946. By this time Tito had consolidated his power in Yugoslavia by ruthlessly rooting out opponents of his Communist regime.

against the Soviet Union and its satellite nations during the 45-year-long post–World War II period known as the Cold War.)

Economic Woes

Yet Yugoslavia's economy didn't exactly flourish. As was the case in other Communist countries, the Yugoslavian government's central planning and control stifled innovation and individual initiative, created inefficiencies in production, and eliminated the essential role that free markets play in determining which goods and services should be produced and what they should cost. A five-year plan designed to rapidly develop Yugoslavia's industrial sector (including motor vehicle and engine manufacturing, shipbuilding, textiles, and food processing) through the introduction of modern technology was typical. The planners failed to anticipate the resources such a goal would require. Lacking sufficient raw materials such as fuel, Yugoslavia had to turn to imports, but it couldn't finance the imports because there was little demand for its sparse and low-quality exports.

Hoping to better the situation, the government introduced a new economic reform in 1965. The reform allowed certain enterprises, such as banks and workers' councils, to keep a larger share of the revenue they made. The government believed this would create a feeling of self-management and give workers incentive to exceed their goals. The reform did increase output, but state-run enterprises eventually cut jobs and reduced wages. Faced with a massive pool of disgruntled citizens, the government started to permit its people to migrate for work—a practice once strongly discouraged as it was viewed as betraying one's country. At this time, many workers took advantage of the government's new "open border" policy and left Yugoslavia to find work elsewhere. By 1971 nearly 800,000 workers had left the country.

In search of employment and better pay, some Yugoslavians migrated to North America. However, most went to Western European countries, such as Germany, Switzerland, and Austria. Once employed, the Yugoslavians remained in these countries as guest workers, often for several years. (A guest worker is a foreigner with a temporary term of employment who does not have a right to stay in the host country permanently.) The Yugoslavian guest workers paid the Yugoslav government a percentage of their wages for the privilege of maintaining their citizenship. Their refusal to cut ties to their homeland was motivated in part by feelings of nationalism, but a more significant reason was that many were supporting families back home in Yugoslavia.

The migration of Yugoslavian guest workers gained momentum

in the early 1970s, when hundreds of thousands held jobs in Western Europe. For the Tito government, whose attempts to breathe life into the Yugoslav economy continued to struggle, this provided an important safety valve. Not only did guest workers remit much-needed funds to their families at home, but their departure also eased unemployment in Yugoslavia.

In 1973, however, Middle Eastern members of the Organization of Petroleum Exporting Countries (OPEC) imposed an oil embargo on the United States and other Western industrialized nations to protest their policies toward Israel and the Arab states. As oil prices skyrocketed, the world economy slumped. This economic recession caused many Western European countries to cut down on the number of foreign workers they would accept.

The oil crisis hit Yugoslavia doubly hard. Not only were dramatically fewer workers able to find employment overseas—

A Macedonian mother and son in the countryside, 1974. Efforts by Yugoslavia's government to create a modern industrial economy met with decidedly mixed results. While workers in the more developed republics of Slovenia and Croatia prospered, those in the poorer republics, including Macedonia, lagged behind. In addition, high unemployment remained a chronic problem.

removing an important support to the Yugoslav economy—but the country's industrial production, which was heavily reliant on imported petroleum, lagged as well. Tito's government borrowed money to keep the economy going. But by 1979, when petroleum prices again spiked and most of the world fell into another recession, Yugoslavia's foreign debt—which had reached nearly $20 billion—became unmanageable.

The 1979 world economic recession once again forced many Yugoslavian guest workers to return home. To deal with this situation, the government pressured its various enterprises to hire as many of the surplus workers as possible. This meant creating new jobs at a time when wages were already low. As a result, the personal income of employees dropped even further. At this time, the average Yugoslavian worker's monthly take-home pay was equivalent to only about $170. But wages varied significantly by republic. For example, in Macedonia, labor-intensive and less profitable industries such as textile manufacturing, agriculture, and handicrafts predominated. Workers in these industries received half of what Slovenian workers in the technology and building production fields were paid. This fostered a great deal of resentment among residents of the less developed republics.

But feelings of resentment weren't limited to people in the poorer republics. Revenue generated by the wealthier republics, such as Croatia and Slovenia, was used to support the rest of the country. Shortly after the economic reforms of the 1960s went into effect, Croatian university students began to discuss the possibility of independence for their republic. Many Croatians believed that, because of their republic's successful tourism industry and relatively large-scale production of export goods, they were paying Yugoslavia's bills. Similar feelings existed among Slovenians. By 1971 Croatian officials in the Communist Party were circulating proposals for the secession, or withdrawal, of Croatia from the Yugoslav federation. At this point Tito stepped in and suppressed the offending groups.

Rising nationalism did lead to some concessions, however. In

1974 Yugoslavia's constitution was modified to give autonomous status to two areas within the borders of the republic of Serbia: Kosovo, an enclave of mostly ethnic Albanians; and Vojvodina, home to many ethnic Hungarians.

Disintegration

To outside observers, it seemed that the only thing holding Yugoslavia together was the iron rule of Josip Broz Tito, and many predicted that nationalism would tear the country apart upon his death. On May 4, 1980, the longtime leader died at the age of 88, but the dire predictions did not materialize—at least not immediately. In part this was because Yugoslavians feared that the Soviet Union might try to exploit any turmoil to bring their country under its control. By the late 1980s, though, this external threat had all but disappeared, as the Soviet Union relinquished control of its Eastern European satellite nations, which one by one cast off their Communist governments. In 1991 the Soviet Union itself collapsed.

By this time events in Yugoslavia were moving inevitably toward disaster. Ten years earlier, in 1981, demonstrations by university students in Kosovo had triggered widespread unrest in that autonomous region. The demonstrators demanded that Kosovo—with its majority ethnic Albanian and Muslim population—be recognized as a full-fledged republic alongside the six others in Yugoslavia. The situation turned bloody when Serb officials, acting in concert with the Yugoslav army, moved to quell the unrest. The Serbs insisted that Kosovo rightfully belonged to the republic of Serbia, and the incident stirred feelings of Serb nationalism.

As the decade progressed, Serb nationalism—manipulated to a great degree by ambitious leaders—turned into extremism. In 1987 a previously obscure official in the Serbian Communist Party, Slobodan Milosevic, gained notoriety by delivering an angry speech in Kosovo during a strike by Kosovar Albanian miners. "You will not be beaten again," Milosevic told a crowd of Serbs, playing to his audience's

Slobodan Milosevic—who, critics charge, rose through the ranks of the Serbian Communist Party largely by stirring up ethnic fears and hatred—is widely blamed for much of the tragedy that befell Yugoslavia.

sense of historical victimization.

Two years later, Milosevic gave another fateful speech in Kosovo—this time at the site of the Battle of Kosovo Polje, on the battle's 600th anniversary. More than a million Serbs were in attendance. Nowhere in the speech did Milosevic specifically call for the repression of Kosovar Albanians or any of Yugoslavia's other ethnic groups; nor did he explicitly advocate the creation of a "Greater Serbia," a republic that would unite all of Yugoslavia's ethnic Serbs. But, many experts suggest, his speech was filled with allusions calculated to inflame Serb nationalist passions. His references to the "betrayal" of the Serbian people and their centuries-long "slavery" under the Ottoman Turks played to Serb grievances against the Kosovar Albanians—converts to Islam who, Serbs believed, had been favored by Ottoman administrators. When Milosevic mentioned "fascist aggression" and the "agony" the Serbian people had suffered in "the last war," many in his audience no doubt recalled how, during World War II, ethnic Albanians had collaborated with Fascist Italian forces—and Croats had joined Nazi Germany—in persecuting the Serbs. And though

Milosevic extolled "equal and harmonious relations among Yugoslav peoples," he also repeatedly warned against the dangers of "disunity" among Serbs and said that "when socialist Yugoslavia was set up . . . [t]he concessions that many Serbian leaders made at the expense of their people could not be accepted historically and ethically by any nation in the world"—an apparent indictment of multiethnic Yugoslavia. Soon the autonomous status of Kosovo and Vojvodina was revoked.

The increasingly strident tone of Serbian nationalism troubled other ethnic groups in Yugoslavia. But nationalism was alive in the other republics as well.

In the spring of 1990, as reforms swept through the nations of Eastern Europe with the pullback of the Soviet Union, Yugoslavia's Communist Party agreed to give up its monopoly on power and hold multiparty parliamentary elections for the first time. Voters in Slovenia and Croatia elected representatives who favored increased sovereignty (or even independence) for their republics. In Serbia, meanwhile, Milosevic's Communist Party, which continued to insist on a strong, centralized government, claimed victory. Communist allies of Milosevic also won in Montenegro. The future of Yugoslavia appeared uncertain, and negotiations to resolve the differences among the various republics led nowhere.

In December 1990, Slovenians overwhelmingly voted for full independence for their republic in a plebiscite (a referendum to determine their political status). A similar result occurred in Croatia.

In early 1991, sporadic fighting broke out between Croats and ethnic Serbs in Croatia. The Croatian Serbs—recalling, perhaps, their persecution by the Ustasha during World War II—were alarmed by the anti-Serb rhetoric of the now-dominant Croatian Democratic Union Party and its leader, Franjo Tudjman. For their part, many Croatian leaders suspected that Serbs from Croatia's Krajina region were planning to unite the area with Serbia.

Matters were not helped when, in May, Slobodan Milosevic and his allies halted an important power-sharing arrangement that had been put in place after the death of Tito. In the post-Tito period, Yugoslavia's presidency had rotated, with a leader from each of the republics serving a one-year term. But now Milosevic—using his influence in the heavily Serb republic of Montenegro and in Kosovo and Vojvodina—blocked Stjepan "Stipe" Mesic, a Croat, from serving as president when it was Mesic's turn. The Federal Republic of Yugoslavia was effectively without a leader.

One month later, on June 25, 1991, Slovenia and Croatia officially declared their independence. Yugoslavia's breakup was now inevitable.

Young Slovenians demonstrate for independence, 1991. Slovenia successfully broke away from Yugoslavia after a brief war. In Croatia, which declared its independence on the same day as Slovenia, the fighting was much more bitter and protracted.

War in Slovenia and Croatia

Shortly after the Slovenian and Croatian declarations of independence, the Serb-dominated Yugoslav federal army moved into Slovenia. The fighting was fierce, if brief. Given the stiffness of the resistance, along with Slovenia's small size and its tiny ethnic Serb population, Serbian officials apparently concluded that a protracted war in Slovenia would not be worth the cost. About 100 people were killed before the sides agreed to a cease-fire brokered by the European Community, and the Yugoslav army withdrew.

Croatia, however, was a different matter. A large republic with an ethnic Serb population of about 12 percent, Croatia became a major battleground. Croatian Serb paramilitary fighters, backed by air force and artillery units of the Yugoslav armed forces, rapidly gained control of the Krajina region. By the end of the year, Serbs held almost one-third of Croatian territory. Thousands of soldiers were killed in the fighting. In addition—in a pattern that would be repeated frequently in the coming years—both sides deliberately drove thousands of people of the other ethnic group from their homes as a means of securing control over territory. This practice would become known euphemistically as "ethnic cleansing." Massacres of civilians also occurred.

By January 1992, a cease-fire was negotiated with the help of the United States. As part of the agreement, United Nations peacekeeping troops entered Croatia. Despite the efforts of the U.N. peacekeepers, fighting erupted again in 1993, in Serb-controlled Krajina. By that time, however, the international focus had shifted to conflict in another Yugoslav republic.

Bosnian Horrors

By early 1992, tensions had been rising for months in Bosnia and Herzegovina. Though Muslims (often referred to as Bosniacs) constituted about 44 percent of the population, Bosnia and Herzegovina was Yugoslavia's most ethnically balanced republic, with a Serb minority of about 31 percent and a

Croat minority of about 17 percent. As the crises in Slovenia and Croatia unfolded, Bosnia and Herzegovina's Muslim-controlled parliament began discussing the possibility of independence for their republic. Bosnian Serbs and Yugoslav federal officials vowed to oppose such a move with force.

Despite these threats, the citizens of Bosnia and Herzegovina voted for independence in a March 1992 referendum boycotted by the republic's Serb population. The following month, after the European Community and the United States recognized Bosnia and Herzegovina as an independent state, Bosnian Serbs proclaimed their own republic inside Bosnia.

In a brutal war that would rage for the next three years, the Bosnian Serbs—aided by the Yugoslav federal army—sought to slice off territory for their self-proclaimed republic. Ethnic cleansing became their primary weapon. Bosnian Serb military units descended on scores of Muslim (and, to a lesser degree, Croat) villages—murdering, raping, looting, and driving off the inhabitants. In all, the war created a million Bosnian refugees.

But the Serb forces had no monopoly on atrocities. Bosnian Muslims also carried out a smaller campaign of ethnic cleansing against Bosnian Serbs. And Croatian troops crossed into Bosnia, sometimes striking Serb civilian enclaves. In addition, while they were generally allied with the Bosnian Muslims against the Bosnian Serbs, until 1994 Bosnian Croats and Croatian army units periodically fought the Bosniacs, for Croatia also had designs on Bosnian territory.

Throughout the war, the international community made various attempts to contain or end the fighting, with mixed results. The United Nations imposed economic sanctions, but they took years to cripple the economies of Serbia and Montenegro. And an arms embargo on all of Yugoslavia disadvantaged the much more poorly equipped Bosnian Muslims.

By mid-1992, the Bosnian Serbs controlled about 70 percent of the territory of Bosnia and Herzegovina, and they were laying siege to the republic's capital, Sarajevo, and threatening other Muslim areas. U.N. peacekeeping troops were sent in to ensure

A Bosnian Serb tank rolls through a village in north-western Bosnia and Herzegovina. The civil war in Yugoslavia's most ethnically balanced republic, which broke out in 1992, was exceptionally brutal.

the flow of humanitarian aid to the besieged populations, but the Serb forces kept up the pressure.

In 1993 the U.N. declared six "safe zones"—Sarajevo, Tuzla, Srebrenica, Gorazde, Bihac, and Zepa—where Bosnian Muslims would supposedly be protected against Serb aggression, but shelling of these areas continued. In March 1994 a mortar attack on a Sarajevo market killed 68 people and wounded more than 200. In response, the North Atlantic Treaty Organization (NATO)—a post–World War II alliance that included the United States, Canada, and Western European countries—began carrying out air strikes against Bosnian Serb positions.

In the spring of 1994, U.S. mediation helped lead to an agreement among the Bosnian Muslim government, the government of Croatia, and the Bosnian Croats. The agreement, which created a Muslim-Croat confederation in Bosnia, effectively ended fighting between the two groups, which now concentrated their efforts against the Bosnian Serbs. This, combined with expanded NATO air strikes, helped convince Slobodan Milosevic to agree to a four-month cease-fire in December.

Unfortunately, the Serbs renewed hostilities after the four months had passed. In July of 1995, Bosnian Serb forces overran the "safe areas" of Srebrenica and Zepa. In Srebrenica, at least 7,500 Muslim men and boys were separated from their families, marched out of the city, and shot. It was the worst massacre Europe had seen since World War II.

As summer progressed, a month-long NATO bombardment and steady gains on the ground by the Muslim-Croat forces finally led the Serbs to agree to another cease-fire. Eventually, in November, the parties signed the Dayton Peace Accords, officially bringing the war to a close. The Dayton Accords kept intact Bosnia and Herzegovina but recognized two autonomous areas within the country: the Bosniac-Croat Federation and the Bosnian Serb Republic.

Leaders of the various groups fighting in Bosnia and Herzegovina (from left: Serbian president Slobodan Milosevic, Bosnian president Alia Izetbegovic, and Croatian president Franjo Tudjman) came together in December 1995 to sign the Dayton Accords.

Crisis in Kosovo

By the late 1990s, all that remained of Yugoslavia were the republics of Serbia and Montenegro. Slovenia, Croatia, and Bosnia and Herzegovina had all gained independence after wars; Macedonia, poor and with a small ethnic Serb population, had separated from Yugoslavia without bloodshed in September 1991 after a referendum on independence. In January 1998 Croatia recaptured the last part of the Serb enclave of Krajina. Dreams of a "Greater Serbia" had evaporated.

But the violence in the region was not quite finished. In Kosovo, where some 90 percent of the people were ethnic Albanians, resentment simmered over Slobodan Milosevic's removal of the province's autonomous status in 1991. Kosovar Albanians complained that the Serb minority was trampling their political rights and trying to suppress their language and culture. In 1997 a small guerrilla group called the Kosovo Liberation Army (KLA) began attacking Serb police. In February 1998, Milosevic dispatched Yugoslav and Serbian troops to root out the KLA, but the brutality of the response spurred fears of ethnic cleansing. Riots broke out in Pristina, Kosovo's capital.

The situation rapidly worsened. As the Yugoslav government launched a full-scale offensive, thousands of Kosovar Albanians fled their villages. Large numbers of recruits joined the KLA, and, armed by the neighboring country of Albania, the rebels stepped up attacks on federal soldiers as well as Serb civilians.

NATO threats to intervene in the growing crisis prompted a cease-fire in the fall, but violence erupted again in early 1999. Determined to avoid a repeat of what happened in Bosnia, NATO set out to impose a peace settlement upon the warring parties—with force if necessary. Though the KLA eventually agreed to accept the settlement, Milosevic refused, instead launching a renewed offensive in Kosovo.

In late March 1999, NATO began an aerial bombardment campaign to compel Yugoslav compliance with its peace plan. The attacks were directed not just at Yugoslav military positions within Kosovo, but also at Yugoslavia proper, including the capital, Belgrade.

Remembering the Horror in Kosovo

On April 14, 1999, Mentor Nimani, a Kosovar Albanian human-rights attorney, testified before the U.S. Senate Immigration Subcommittee. The subcommittee was holding hearings on atrocities in Kosovo. The following are excerpts from Nimani's testimony:

On March 25, the day after the [NATO] bombing started, I received a call from my boss in Belgrade who I prefer to leave unnamed. She had received a call from Bajram Keljmendi's wife informing her that Bajram and their two sons had been taken from their home in the middle of the night by a group of armed men in black uniforms with police insignias. Their bodies were found several days later. They had been shot. Bajram's sons were my close friends.

. . . In Tirana, I began to talk to other refugees and document their stories. They spoke to me of the ordeals they had suffered and the atrocities they had witnessed. I spoke to one group of refugees from Peja. They told me that Serb authorities had expelled them from Kosovo and ordered them to walk to Albania. The men were separated from the women and they were threatened with death if they did not come up with money. To spare the men, the group gave the authorities all their money. On the way to Albania, two children and an elderly woman died. The group traveled without food or water. But, their worst experience was when they reached the border. There, Serb authorities forced them to stay the night. While they were trying to sleep in the open, loud speakers played. On the loud speakers they heard the voices of children screaming as if they were being killed. They also heard continuous threats of atrocities that would be committed against them, including descriptions of how they would be killed. One woman I spoke with said that this was the worst experience of her life. She will never be able to recover from this.

Another man and woman from Gakova described their escape from that city. Soldiers shot at them as they fled. They believe that eighty percent of the city has been set on fire and destroyed. In one mosque they passed in Gakova as they fled, they saw as many as 300 bodies of people slain.

Unfortunately, during the 11 weeks of the NATO air strikes, Yugoslav and Serb forces on the ground undertook another horrific campaign of ethnic cleansing. The soldiers executed thousands of Kosovar Albanians, systematically raped women and girls, and drove hundreds of thousands of people from their homes. All told, an estimated 900,000 refugees and internally displaced persons were forced from their homes in Kosovo during the NATO bombing campaign, according to the United Nations High Commissioner for Refugees. Most of the refugees went to Albania, Macedonia, and Montenegro. The United States accepted approximately 20,000 Kosovar refugees. In many cases, they were airlifted from the region.

In early June, Milosevic finally agreed to withdraw all his troops from Kosovo and to accept a NATO peacekeeping force there. The air strikes were suspended.

The Demise of Slobodan Milosevic and the End of Yugoslavia

Having led his now-impoverished country into a disastrous series of wars, Slobodan Milosevic saw his popularity fall after the Kosovo conflict. In presidential elections held in September 2000, an opposition candidate, Vojislav Kostunica, won an overwhelming majority. Milosevic initially refused to accept the results, but after massive protests in the streets of Belgrade, he finally stepped aside. Arrested in 2001, he was later sent to The Hague to face war crimes charges before the United Nations–sponsored International Criminal Tribunal for the Former Yugoslavia. The trial was still in progress as of summer 2003.

By that time, the vestiges of Yugoslavia were gone. In February 2003, Serbia and Montenegro agreed to a looser confederation. Referenda scheduled for 2006 are likely to produce full independence for both republics.

3 YUGOSLAVIAN IMMIGRATION TO NORTH AMERICA

During the last half of the 20th century, Yugoslavia experienced conditions that typically cause people to think about leaving their homes to start a new life in another land: a weak economy, political instability, war. But emigrants from the region had settled in North America before then—a significant number of them during the 19th century. Of course, as the country of Yugoslavia did not then exist, these people did not regard themselves as Yugoslavians but as Croats, Serbs, Montenegrins, Macedonians, Slovenes, or Bosnians. And even after Yugoslavia had been created, many immigrants continued to identify more with their ethnic group than with their country.

It is estimated that, in the two-decade period between the end of World War I and the beginning of World II (1919–1939), more than 80,000 immigrants from Yugoslavia were admitted to North America. More than 30,000 of them settled in Canada, while an additional 50,000 settled in the United States. Many of these immigrants were ethnic Slavs. But many others were of Austrian or Italian ancestry. When boundaries were redrawn after the First World War, these people found themselves in the unwanted position of living as ethnic minorities in a newly created country. Yet all immigrants from Yugoslavia, Slavic or otherwise, were counted as Yugoslavians.

After World War II, when Marshal Tito took control of Yugoslavia and made it a Communist country, the flow of

◀ A family of Kosovar refugees in Albania, 1999. The crisis in Kosovo displaced about 900,000 people, and NATO member countries agreed to take in refugees to avoid a humanitarian catastrophe. The United States agreed to accept 20,000 Kosovar refugees; Canada, 5,000.

emigrants ceased. Tito viewed emigration unfavorably, and his government made it extremely difficult for citizens to leave the country. It was also hard for foreigners to enter. This closed-border policy dominated postwar Yugoslavia for about 15 years.

By the early 1960s, however, Yugoslavia's economy was foundering under a large international debt and growing unemployment. After a series of failed laws, the government introduced the Economic Reform Act of 1965. This new law devalued Yugoslavia's currency so that foreign companies and entrepreneurs could invest more of their money in the country's industries. In addition, it reduced tariffs and import restrictions. The act also called for an easing of travel limitations to and from Yugoslavia, which not only brought in more money through tourism, but also solved part of the unemployment problem by allowing Yugoslav citizens to work abroad.

Most Yugoslavians seeking work abroad headed to Western Europe. However, some saw the new open-border policy as an opportunity to travel much farther, setting their sights on North America. By chance, immigration laws in the United States and Canada were changing around this same time. Barriers that had been erected to keep out members of unwanted groups were coming down.

U.S. Immigration Policy to 1965

Immigration to the United States has been characterized by openness punctuated by periods of restriction. During the 17th, 18th, and 19th centuries, immigration was essentially open without restriction, and, at times, immigrants were even recruited to come to America. Between 1783 and 1820, approximately 250,000 immigrants arrived at U.S. shores. Between 1841 and 1860, more than 4 million immigrants came; most were from England, Ireland, and Germany.

Historically, race and ethnicity have played a role in legislation to restrict immigration. The Chinese Exclusion Act of 1882, which was not repealed until 1943, specifically prevent-

Immigrants have not always been welcomed into the United States. This cartoon, published in 1881 in the San Francisco–based magazine the *Wasp*, attributes a host of social ills, including immorality, disease, filth, and the ruin of "white labor," to Chinese immigrants. The following year, Congress passed the Chinese Exclusion Act of 1882, which cut off immigration from China.

ed Chinese people from becoming U.S. citizens and did not allow Chinese laborers to immigrate for the next decade. An agreement with Japan in the early 1900s prevented most Japanese immigration to the United States.

Until the 1920s, no numerical restrictions on immigration existed in the United States, although health restrictions applied. The only other significant restrictions came in 1917, when passing a literacy test became a requirement for immigrants. Presidents Cleveland, Taft, and Wilson had vetoed similar measures earlier. In addition, in 1917 a prohibition was added to the law against the immigration of people from Asia (defined as the Asiatic barred zone). While a few of these prohibitions were lifted during World War II, they were not repealed until 1952, and even then Asians were only allowed in under very small annual quotas.

During World War I, the federal government required that all travelers to the United States obtain a visa at a U.S. consulate or diplomatic post abroad. As former State Department consular affairs officer C. D. Scully points out, by making that requirement permanent Congress, by 1924, established the framework of temporary, or non-immigrant visas (for study, work, or travel), and immigrant visas (for permanent residence). That framework remains in place today.

After World War I, cultural intolerance and bizarre racial theories led to new immigration restrictions. The House Judiciary Committee employed a eugenics consultant, Dr. Harry N. Laughlin, who asserted that certain races were inferior. Another leader of the eugenics movement, Madison Grant, argued that Jews, Italians, and others were inferior because of their supposedly different skull size.

The Immigration Act of 1924, preceded by the Temporary Quota Act of 1921, set new numerical limits on immigration based on "national origin." Taking effect in 1929, the 1924 act set annual quotas on immigrants that were specifically designed to keep out southern Europeans, such as Italians and Greeks. Generally no more than 100 people of the proscribed nationalities were permitted to immigrate.

While the new law was rigid, the U.S. Department of State's restrictive interpretation directed consular officers overseas to be even stricter in their application of the "public charge" provision. (A public charge is someone unable to support himself or his family.) As author Laura Fermi wrote, "In response to the new cry for restriction at the beginning of the [Great Depression] . . . the consuls were to interpret very strictly the clause prohibiting admission of aliens 'likely to become public charges; and to deny the visa to an applicant who in their opinion might become a public charge at any time.'"

In the early 1900s, more than one million immigrants a year came to the United States. In 1930—the first year of the national-origin quotas—approximately 241,700 immigrants were admitted. But under the State Department's strict interpretations, only 23,068 immigrants entered during 1933, the smallest total since 1831. Later these restrictions prevented many Jews in

Germany and elsewhere in Europe from escaping what would become the Holocaust. At the height of the Holocaust in 1943, the United States admitted fewer than 6,000 refugees.

The Displaced Persons Act of 1948, the nation's first refugee law, allowed many refugees from World War II to settle in the United States. The law put into place policy changes that had already seen immigration rise from 38,119 in 1945 to 108,721 in 1946 (and later to 249,187 in 1950). One-third of those admitted between 1948 and 1951 were Poles, with ethnic Germans forming the second-largest group.

The 1952 Immigration and Nationality Act is best known for its restrictions against those who supported communism or anarchy. However, the bill's other provisions were quite restrictive and were passed over the veto of President Truman. The 1952 act retained the national-origin quota system for the Eastern Hemisphere. The Western Hemisphere continued to operate without a quota and relied on other qualitative factors to limit immigration. Moreover, during that time, the Mexican

President Lyndon B. Johnson at his desk in the Oval Office. Upon signing into law the Immigration Act of 1965, President Johnson declared that the national-origin quota system would "never again shadow the gate to the American nation with the twin barriers of prejudice and privilege."

bracero program, from 1942 to 1964, allowed millions of Mexican agricultural workers to work temporarily in the United States.

The 1952 act set aside half of each national quota to be divided among three preference categories for relatives of U.S. citizens and permanent residents. The other half went to aliens with high education or exceptional abilities. These quotas applied only to those from the Eastern Hemisphere.

A Halt to the National-Origin Quotas

The Immigration and Nationality Act of 1965 became a landmark in immigration legislation by specifically striking the racially based national-origin quotas. It removed the barriers to Asian immigration, which later led to opportunities to immigrate for many Filipinos, Chinese, Koreans, and others. The Western Hemisphere was designated a ceiling of 120,000 immigrants but without a preference system or per country limits. Modifications made in 1978 ultimately combined the Western and Eastern Hemispheres into one preference system and one ceiling of 290,000.

The 1965 act built on the existing system—without the national-origin quotas—and gave somewhat more priority to family relationships. It did not completely overturn the existing system but rather carried forward essentially intact the family immigration categories from the 1959 amendments to the Immigration and Nationality Act. Even though the text of the law prior to 1965 indicated that half of the immigration slots were reserved for skilled employment immigration, in practice, Immigration and Naturalization Service (INS) statistics show that 86 percent of the visas issued between 1952 and 1965 went for family immigration.

A number of significant pieces of legislation since 1980 have shaped the current U.S. immigration system. First, the Refugee Act of 1980 removed refugees from the annual world limit for immigration. The act also established that the president would set the number of refugees who could be admitted each year after consultations with Congress.

Second, the 1986 Immigration Reform and Control Act (IRCA) introduced sanctions against employers who "knowingly" hired undocumented immigrants (those here illegally). It also provided amnesty for many undocumented immigrants.

Third, the Immigration Act of 1990 increased legal immigration by 40 percent. In particular, the act significantly increased the number of employment-based immigrants (to 140,000), while also boosting family immigration.

Fourth, the 1996 Illegal Immigration Reform and Immigrant Responsibility Act (IIRAIRA) significantly tightened rules that permitted undocumented immigrants to convert to legal status and made other changes that tightened immigration law in areas such as political asylum and deportation.

Fifth, in response to the September 11, 2001, terrorist attacks, the USA PATRIOT Act and the Enhanced Border Security and Visa Entry Reform Act tightened rules on the granting of visas to individuals from certain countries and enhanced the federal government's monitoring and detention authority over foreign nationals in the United States.

New U.S. Immigration Agencies

In a dramatic reorganization of the federal government, the Homeland Security Act of 2002 abolished the Immigration and Naturalization Service and transferred its immigration service and enforcement functions from the Department of Justice into a new Department of Homeland Security. The Customs Service, the Coast Guard, and parts of other agencies were also transferred into the new department.

The Department of Homeland Security, with regards to immigration, is organized as follows: The Bureau of Customs and Border Protection (BCBP) contains Customs and Immigration inspectors, who check the documents of travelers to the United States at air, sea, and land ports of entry; and Border Patrol agents, the uniformed agents who seek to prevent unlawful entry along the southern and northern border. The new Bureau

of Immigration and Customs Enforcement (BICE) employs investigators, who attempt to find undocumented immigrants inside the United States, and Detention and Removal officers, who detain and seek to deport such individuals. The new Bureau of Citizenship and Immigration Services (BCIS) is where people go, or correspond with, to become U.S. citizens or obtain permission to work or extend their stay in the United States.

As members of Congress look on, President George W. Bush signs the Enhanced Border Security and Visa Entry Reform Act, May 14, 2002.

Following the terrorist attacks of September 11, 2001, the Department of Justice adopted several measures that did not require new legislation to be passed by Congress. Some of these measures created controversy and raised concerns about civil liberties. For example, FBI and INS agents detained for months more than 1,000 foreign nationals of Middle Eastern descent and refused to release the names of the individuals. It is alleged that the Department of Justice adopted tactics that discouraged the detainees from obtaining legal assistance. The Department of Justice also began requiring foreign nationals from primarily Muslim nations to be fingerprinted and questioned by immigration officers upon entry or if they have been living in the

United States. Those involved in the September 11 attacks were not immigrants—people who become permanent residents with a right to stay in the United States—but holders of temporary visas, primarily visitor or tourist visas.

Today, the annual rate of legal immigration is lower than that at earlier periods in U.S. history. For example, from 1901 to 1910 approximately 10.4 immigrants per 1,000 U.S. residents came to the United States. Today, the annual rate is about 3.5 immigrants per 1,000 U.S. residents. While the percentage of foreign-born people in the U.S. population has risen above 11 percent, it remains lower than the 13 percent or higher that prevailed in the country from 1860 to 1930. Still, as has been the case previously in U.S. history, some people argue that even legal immigration should be lowered. These people maintain that immigrants take jobs native-born Americans could fill and that U.S. population growth, which immigration contributes to, harms the environment. In 1996 Congress voted against efforts to reduce legal immigration.

Most immigrants (800,000 to one million annually) enter the United States legally. But over the years the undocumented (illegal) portion of the population has increased to about 2.8 percent of the U.S. population—approximately 8 million people in all.

Today, the legal immigration system in the United States contains many rules, permitting only individuals who fit into certain categories to immigrate—and in many cases only after waiting anywhere from 1 to 10 years or more, depending on the demand in that category. The system, representing a compromise among family, employment, and human rights concerns, has the following elements:

A U.S. citizen may sponsor for immigration a spouse, parent, sibling, or minor or adult child.

A lawful permanent resident (green card holder) may sponsor only a spouse or child.

A foreign national may immigrate if he or she gains an employer sponsor.

An individual who can show that he or she has a "well-founded fear of persecution" may come to the country as a refugee—or be allowed to stay as an asylee (someone who receives asylum).

Beyond these categories, essentially the only other way to immigrate is to apply for and receive one of the "diversity" visas, which are granted annually by lottery to those from "underrepresented" countries.

In 1996 changes to the law prohibited nearly all incoming immigrants from being eligible for federal public benefits, such as welfare, during their first five years in the country. Refugees were mostly excluded from these changes. In addition, families who sponsor relatives must sign an affidavit of support showing they can financially take care of an immigrant who falls on hard times.

A Short History of Canadian Immigration

In the 1800s, immigration into Canada was largely unrestricted. Farmers and artisans from England and Ireland made up a significant portion of 19th-century immigrants. England's Parliament passed laws that facilitated and encouraged the voyage to North America, particularly for the poor.

After the United States barred Chinese railroad workers from settling in the country, Canada encouraged the immigration of Chinese laborers to assist in the building of Canadian railways. Responding to the racial views of the time, the Canadian Parliament began charging a "head tax" for Chinese and South Asian (Indian) immigrants in 1885. The fee of $50—later raised to $500—was well beyond the means of laborers making one or two dollars a day. Later, the government sought additional ways to prohibit Asians from entering the country. For example, it decided to require a "continuous journey," meaning that immigrants to Canada had to travel from their country on a boat that made an uninterrupted passage. For immigrants or asylum seekers from Asia this was nearly impossible.

As the 20th century progressed, concerns about race led to further restrictions on immigration to Canada. These restrictions particularly hurt Jewish and other refugees seeking to flee persecution in Europe. Government statistics indicate that Canada accepted no more than 5,000 Jewish refugees before and during the Holocaust.

After World War II, Canada, like the United States, began accepting thousands of Europeans displaced by the war. Canada's laws were modified to accept these war refugees, as well as Hungarians fleeing Communist authorities after the crushing of the 1956 Hungarian Revolution.

The Immigration Act of 1952 in Canada allowed for a "tap on, tap off" approach to immigration, granting administrative authorities the power to allow more immigrants into the coun-

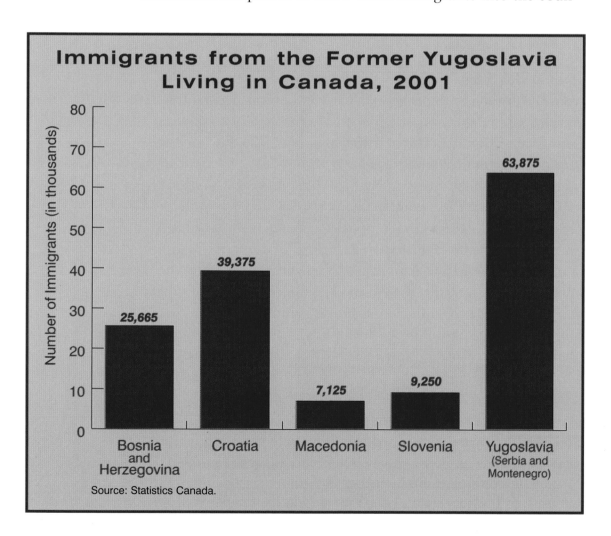

Immigrants from the Former Yugoslavia Living in Canada, 2001

Source: Statistics Canada.

try in good economic times, and fewer in times of recession. The shortcoming of such an approach is that there is little evidence immigrants harm a national economy and much evidence they contribute to economic growth, particularly in the growth of the labor force.

In 1966 the government of Prime Minister Lester Pearson introduced a policy statement stressing how immigrants were key to Canada's economic growth. With Canada's relatively small population base, it became clear that in the absence of newcomers, the country would not be able to grow. The policy was introduced four years after Parliament enacted important legislation that eliminated Canada's own version of racially based national-origin quotas.

In 1967 a new law established a points system that awarded entry to potential immigrants using criteria based primarily on an individual's age, language ability, skills, education, family relationships, and job prospects. The total points needed for entry of an immigrant is set by the Minister of Citizenship and Immigration Canada. The new law also established a category for humanitarian (refugee) entry.

The 1976 Immigration Act refined and expanded the possibility for entry under the points system, particularly for individuals seeking to sponsor family members. The act also expanded refugee and asylum law to comport with Canada's international obligations. The law established five basic categories for immigration into Canada: 1) family; 2) humanitarian; 3) independents (including skilled workers), who immigrate to Canada on their own; 4) assisted relatives; and 5) business immigrants (including investors, entrepreneurs, and the self-employed).

The new Immigration and Refugee Protection Act, which took effect June 28, 2002, made a series of modifications to existing Canadian immigration law. The act, and the regulations that followed, toughened rules on those seeking asylum and the process for removing people unlawfully in Canada.

The law modified the points system, adding greater flexibility for skilled immigrants and temporary workers to become permanent residents, and evaluating skilled workers on the weight of their transferable skills as well as those of their specific occupation. The legislation also made it easier for employers to have a labor shortage declared in an industry or sector, which would facilitate the entry of foreign workers in that industry or sector.

On family immigration, the act permitted parents to sponsor dependent children up to the age of 22 (previously 19 was the maximum age at which a child could be sponsored for immigration). The act also allowed partners in common-law arrangements, including same-sex partners, to be considered as family members for the purpose of immigration sponsorship. Along with these liberalizing measures, the act also included provisions to address perceived gaps in immigration-law enforcement.

Economic Considerations: Yugoslavian Immigration to North America in the 1960s and 1970s

Between 1965 and 1970, after Yugoslavia had dropped its closed-border policy and the United States had abolished its national-origin immigration quotas, more than 16,000 Yugoslavians took advantage of the new opportunity and immigrated to the United States. Economic considerations were a major factor for many in this group. Over the same 1965–1970 period, Canada saw an influx of more than 19,000 Yugoslavian immigrants—not only a larger total than the United States welcomed but also, given Canada's much smaller population, a significantly larger proportion.

In the early 1970s, however, Yugoslavian officials began to rethink their emigration policy after discovering that the majority of those leaving the country for employment purposes were skilled and educated workers—not peasants, as the government had hoped. This left Yugoslavia with a large pool of untrained workers who were unsuited for the high-skill industrial jobs that the country's economic-development plans emphasized. As a result, Tito decided to limit the outflow of skilled workers. In 1973 the Yugoslav government passed legislation that barred citizens from working abroad if an equivalent job existed in Yugoslavia. In addition, potential emigrants were required to complete military service and provide for all children they intended to leave behind before they would be permitted to leave the country.

Worldwide economic conditions also put a brake on Yugoslavian emigration during the 1970s. The oil crises of 1973 and 1979 took a toll on the economies of the industrialized nations, creating high inflation and unemployment. This made immigration to these countries a riskier and less attractive option for Yugoslav workers. In addition, starting in 1974, all the Western European countries that hosted large numbers of guest workers began to severely curtail the number of new workers they would accept, and to encourage guest workers already in the country to return home. Unfortunately, as Yugoslav workers flocked back to their homeland, they encountered rising levels of unemployment there.

In the United States, immigration from Yugoslavia, which had been on the rise since the mid-1960s, topped out at about 5,200 in 1973, when the first oil crisis began to wreak havoc on the economy. By 1979—when the second oil crisis struck—annual immigration from Yugoslavia had shrunk to about 1,900.

Canada's economy was also hit hard by the oil crises of the 1970s. A significant rise in unemployment, combined with increases in the cost of living, made potential immigrants from all parts of the world think twice about moving to Canada, and Yugoslavians were no exception. In 1970 Canada recorded 5,672 newcomers from Yugoslavia. By 1979, however, that number had shrunk to a mere 887.

Calm Before the Storm: The 1980s

Yugoslavia's economic woes continued into the 1980s, though there were a few bright spots. Foreign investment rose, and the country was able to pay down a small portion of its debt. But more significant was an upswing in tourism: millions of people vacationed in Yugoslavia during the 1980s, providing jobs for workers in the hotel, restaurant, and associated industries. Overall, Croatia was the favorite destination of foreign travelers and hence reaped the lion's share of the tourist industry's benefits, though Sarajevo did host the 1984 Winter Olympics, giving Bosnia a substantial, if short-term, economic boost.

The opening ceremony of the 1984 Winter Olympics in Sarajevo. The Sarajevo Games provided Bosnia and Herzegovina with an economic boost and seemed to highlight to the world a progressive and harmonious Yugoslavian society. That illusion would soon be shattered.

Although the U.S. economy emerged from recession in 1983 and began a period of extended growth, immigration from

A Bosnian Refugee's Story

Mina Kovacevic, a Bosnian Muslim from Sarajevo, shared the following story with the U.S. Committee for Refugees:

In May, 1992, two months after the war began, I left my home and homeland. My family's home was directly across the street from a military barracks commandeered by Serbian soldiers. From my window, I could see tanks striking other parts of the city. I could see soldiers coming and going and snipers firing from windows. I could see and hear the shelling. Many of my neighbors were killed. My mother, father, two sisters, nephew, and I spent 24 hours a day in a bomb shelter. We were among 40 people—mostly women and children—hiding in a small, dark room, listening to the shooting and shelling. My sister had been undergoing chemotherapy. But we knew that even if we got her to the hospital, there would be no treatment for her, as the hospital was already overburdened with so many wounded and dying. So we decided to try to leave.

Our car and others were stopped by Serb soldiers. They ordered us to pull off to the side of the road and told us we were being held as hostages. The soldiers began making lists of the children in our convoy, threatening to kill them first. We spent three nights in our car without food.

Along with a few other older men, my father was lined up by soldiers who were going to take the men away. The soldiers then began forcing the elderly men into a sort of refrigerated truck—one used for hauling meat. I feared that if my father left us, we would never see him again. I started running towards my father. Soldiers shouted at me that they would kill me if I didn't stop. But I ran to the commander and begged him to let my dad go. I finally convinced him to do so.

We spent two or three more nights there in the car. We saw and heard the men in the truck being tortured by the soldiers. At night the soldiers would shine flashlights into our cars while bragging of all the children they had already killed. We were all in terror for my 4-year-old nephew.

Yugoslavia remained at low levels during the 1980s. Between 1981 and 1990, a total of 18,762 Yugoslav immigrants were

Finally, we were allowed to go. When we reached Croatia, the Croats put us into a refugee camp where we lived 40 people to a tent. The Croats were not prepared to receive so many people, and after ten days, they told us we had to move on to another camp. . . .

We were the first refugees to arrive in this camp. There were a few huts, and we were lucky enough to be put into one, though we shared it with 12 or 14 strangers. We felt much safer because there was no shooting in the area. But as summer turned into autumn, more refugees arrived. The huts were full, so new arrivals were housed in tents—in rain, snow, and extreme cold—without any heat. Sanitation was deplorable; 20 to 30 toilets and only 20 showers for 3,000 people.

I was the only person in the camp who could speak English, so I was soon working as a volunteer translator for the International Committee of the Red Cross (ICRC). I was glad to help, though I was depressed by the conditions in the camp and frightened for my father, who was taken by the Croat soldiers for two or three days at a time for questioning. I dreamt about continuing my education. I would not be able to attend a Croatian university, since I was not a Croat, and I had no money to pay for schooling.

Then one day, some of the people for whom I had worked in the ICRC found out that a few scholarships were available in the United States for Bosnian students. The greatest thing I could imagine happened to me. I was awarded a scholarship at La Roche College in Pittsburgh, where after three years, I received my B.A. in psychology in 1996.

I have since moved on to graduate studies at the Catholic University of America in Washington, D.C. No longer at the mercy of destiny, I can now plan my future. That means that if the situation in the former Yugoslavia remains stable, I will return to my homeland at the conclusion of my studies and be reunited with my family who are now in Denmark.

admitted to the United States. By way of comparison, more than 1.6 million Mexicans settled legally in the United States during the same period.

Canada did not rebound from its economic recession as quickly as the United States. In 1983 more than 1.5 million Canadians—11.9 percent of the workforce—were unemployed, and the unemployment rate didn't dip below 8 percent until 1998. These unfavorable economic conditions did little to lure immigrants to Canadian shores. In 1981 only 661 Yugoslavians immigrated to Canada; by 1984 that number had fallen to 465. By decade's end, the annual total had rebounded to a little more than 2,000, but that was less than half the number of Yugoslavians who had moved to Canada 20 years earlier, in 1970.

The Effects of War

As Yugoslavia descended into ethnic violence and civil war in the early 1990s, the number of people leaving the country—whether as voluntary emigrants or as refugees (people fleeing grave danger)—exploded. Most ended up in nearby Balkan countries or in Western Europe, but significant numbers also came to North America.

In 1992—after the United States officially recognized the breakaway republics of Slovenia, Croatia, and Bosnia and Herzegovina as independent states—U.S. immigration statistics for the first time began tracking the number of newcomers from the different regions of Yugoslavia. Not surprisingly, there is a strong correlation between the level of violence (and, to a lesser extent, economic conditions) and the number of people who came from a particular republic or region. For example, the number of immigrants from Slovenia—a prosperous republic that had a relatively easy time gaining independence from the Yugoslav federation—never surpassed double digits. In 2000, the peak year for Slovenian immigration to the United States, just 76 individuals arrived.

Croatia, which was also economically prosperous, experienced more violence than Slovenia. But people displaced by the fighting tended to settle in areas under the control of their ethnic group—Croats in the two-thirds of the country the Croatian government held, Croatian Serbs in the Krajina area or in Serbia proper. Hence, while Croatian immigration to the United States rose over the course of the 1990s, the total numbers remained relatively low. U.S. immigration statistics record 77 new Croatian arrivals in 1992, after the civil war had broken out, and 1,078 in 2000.

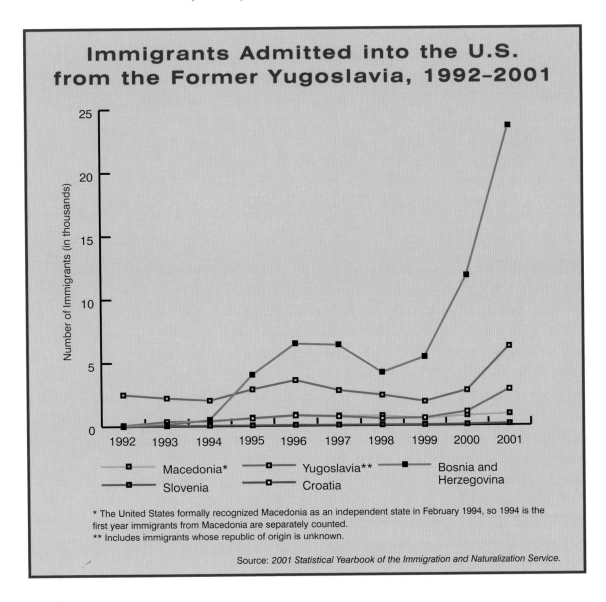

Immigrants Admitted into the U.S. from the Former Yugoslavia, 1992–2001

Legend: Macedonia*, Yugoslavia**, Bosnia and Herzegovina, Slovenia, Croatia

* The United States formally recognized Macedonia as an independent state in February 1994, so 1994 is the first year immigrants from Macedonia are separately counted.
** Includes immigrants whose republic of origin is unknown.

Source: *2001 Statistical Yearbook of the Immigration and Naturalization Service.*

Macedonia's first appearance in the U.S. immigration statistics occurred in 1994. (Although Macedonia had proclaimed its independence in 1991, a dispute with Greece over the country's name delayed United Nations and U.S. recognition.) Macedonia's independence came without bloodshed, and even though it had been Yugoslavia's least developed republic, the country did not send many immigrants to the United States. In 1994 a total of 367 Macedonian immigrants were admitted into the United States. Two years later, the number stood at 863; in 2000 the United States recorded 794 Macedonian newcomers.

Immigration to the United States from Bosnia and Herzegovina, where violence and ethnic cleansing were particularly brutal, increased dramatically in the decade following the outbreak of the civil war. Just 15 Bosnian immigrants came to the United States in 1992, but by 1996 that number had risen to 6,499. And in 2001 the United States admitted 23,640 Bosnian immigrants. In all, during the 10-year period following Bosnia and Herzegovina's 1992 declaration of independence, nearly 63,000 Bosnian immigrants settled in the United States.

But the immigrants are only part of the story. In fact, a far greater number of Bosnians came to the United States as refugees: by the year 2000 more than 100,000 Bosnian refugees were living within U.S. borders, according to the United Nations High Commissioner for Refugees (UNHCR). And in 2001, the U.S. Immigration and Naturalization Service reported, an additional 14,593 Bosnian refugees were accepted into the country. That year, Bosnia and Herzegovina was the largest source country for refugees admitted into the United States, accounting for 21 percent of the U.S. total.

Annual U.S. immigration limits do not apply to refugees, who enter the country through special procedures. To be considered a legal refugee under international law, a person must have fled his or her country because of a "well-founded fear" of persecution based on race, religion, nationality, social group, or political opinion. Bosnians facing ethnic cleansing certainly qualified under this definition.

Ideally, refugees return voluntarily to their home country after the danger to their safety has passed—for example, after a civil war is over. With refugees who might remain vulnerable if they returned home, the UNHCR attempts to have them settled permanently in the country of asylum. When that is not possible (because the country of asylum will not agree to it, for instance), resettlement in a third country is considered. The UNHCR refers only about 1 percent of all refugees for third-country resettlement. Ten countries, including the United States and Canada, have resettlement programs.

The U.S. Refugee Resettlement Program—which is overseen by the State Department's Bureau for Population, Refugees and Migration—considers only those who have been referred by the UNHCR or by the U.S. embassy in the country of asylum. An immigration official interviews these people in the country of asylum and accepts or rejects their application. Those who are accepted are matched with a nonprofit resettlement organization (there are 10 such organizations in the United States), which helps refugees with living arrangements and social services upon their arrival in the country.

The U.S. Committee for Refugees estimated that as of 1996, almost half of Bosnia and Herzegovina's prewar population of 4.4 million was uprooted. Germany alone had granted asylum to as many as 350,000 Bosnian refugees. But after the signing of the Dayton Accords, Germany began repatriating refugees. Though peace had technically been restored to Bosnia and Herzegovina, ethnic violence lingered, and the United States accepted for third-country resettlement many of the refugees who would have been repatriated.

Later in the decade, the United States accepted 20,000 Kosovar refugees under extraordinary circumstances. By early April 1999, after Serb forces unleashed their furious campaign of ethnic cleansing in Kosovo, hundreds of thousands of Kosovar Albanians were trapped in muddy encampments along the borders with Macedonia and Albania. Many had no food or shelter and were exhausted from days of walking. A humanitarian catastrophe loomed. NATO, which two weeks earlier had initiated its bombing campaign to force Yugoslavia to accept a Kosovo peace settlement, decided to airlift refugees directly from the encampments. NATO member countries agreed to take in varying numbers of refugees. Germany, for example, decided to accept 40,000, while the United States and Turkey each offered to take 20,000. Canada accepted 5,000 Kosovar refugees. Because of concerns that removing the refugees would fulfill Slobodan Milosevic's goal of ethnically cleansing Kosovo, NATO officials emphasized that the airlift was an emergency measure, and that the refugees would be returned to their homeland as soon as peace there had been restored.

For 4,000 Kosovar Albanian refugees flown to the United States aboard charter planes throughout the month of May, the first stop was Fort Dix, an army base in New Jersey. There, after being processed, the refugees settled into dorm-like bar-

A Serb man stands in front of the ruins of his house, which was destroyed by a NATO air strike. NATO's 11-week bombing campaign against Serbia and Montenegro ultimately forced Yugoslavian officials to halt the war in Kosovo.

racks in one of two camps set up like villages. Army personnel provided necessary services, and donations of food, clothing, and toys came in from around the United States. By mid-July, all the refugees had been resettled with host families throughout the country.

Yugoslavian Immigration to Canada

Although Canada in the 1990s adopted generally pro-immigration policies—for instance, by increasing the annual immigration ceiling from 200,000 in 1990 to 250,000 in 1992—many individuals still found it difficult to move to the country. Canada's points system favored immigrants who could be expected to contribute to the country's economy, such as those with occupational skills in key industries or entrepreneurs coming to Canada to start a business. By contrast, immigration for the purpose of family reunification was made more difficult; in 1993, for example, Canadian immigration policy reduced the number of preference points awarded to "assisted relatives" (potential immigrants with family members who were already residents of Canada and who agreed to be financially responsible for the newcomers). In addition, the government imposed the Right of Landing Fee in 1995, which required all adults, including refugees, who wanted to establish permanent residence in Canada to pay a $975 admission fee. For those with little means, this fee could be prohibitive.

In 1997, however, the Canadian government introduced the Humanitarian Designated Classes, which provided for the resettlement of persecuted people who still lived in their home country. Included in the list of countries where people would fall under such a category were Croatia and Bosnia and Herzegovina. Approximately 3,670 refugees made their way to Canada under this rule in 1997, a number that gradually decreased to 839 by the year 2000.

4 STARTING A NEW LIFE

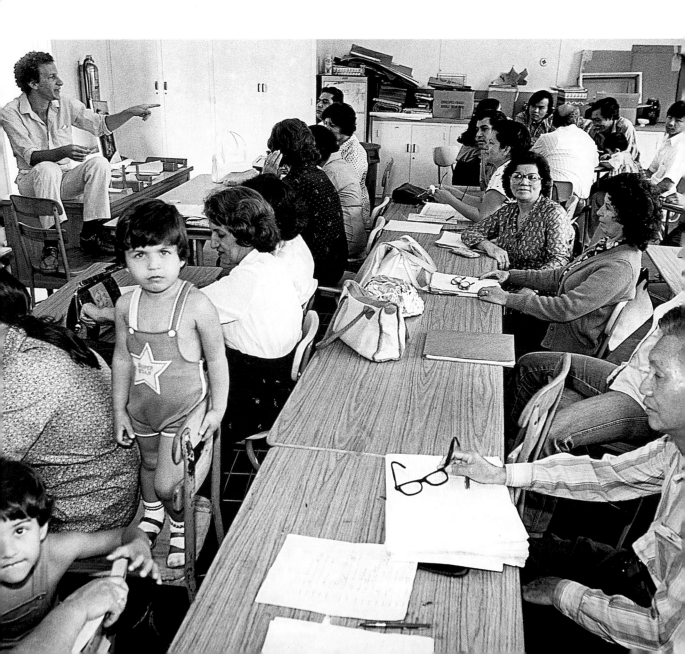

Under the best of circumstances, leaving one's country—with its familiar customs, people, and places—to settle in another land can be a daunting experience. The challenges are multiplied when the immigrant does not know the language of his or her new country, as is the case for many who come to North America from the former Yugoslavia.

Helping Hands

Like other immigrants to the United States and Canada, people hailing from the former Yugoslavia frequently rely on a variety of resources to ease the difficult transition. In the United States, no official welcome is extended to immigrants, though in many communities private organizations provide aid and essential information to newcomers. Language instruction is widely available (though not free) through community colleges. In many cases immigrants from the former Yugoslavia can also turn to an ethnically based organization for help. For example, the Slovene National Benefit Society in Pennsylvania offers business loans, life insurance, and health insurance, among other services. Such organizations help familiarize immigrants with their options and prepare for the future. Not surprisingly, these organizations are most active in areas that have large communities of the particular ethnic group.

Canada offers a more organized and extensive welcome to immigrants. Its Host Program matches immigrants with volun-

◀ An English as a Second Language (ESL) class in Los Angeles. ESL helps immigrants to the United States learn the language of their new home. A similar program, Language Instruction for Newcomers to Canada (LINC), is free for immigrants to Canada.

teer families who show the newcomers around their community. Settlement, or immigration aid, agencies in various Canadian provinces provide immigrants with valuable advice about how to find a permanent place to live and where to buy food, furniture, and clothing at low cost. These agencies also supply immigrants with basic yet essential information, such as how to use public transportation, where to exchange money, how to use postal services, and where to find community centers and libraries. A few settlement agencies help immigrants find jobs. Most services provided by settlement agencies are free. Canada also provides immigrants, at no cost, Language Instruction for Newcomers to Canada (LINC). LINC classes, which may last from several months to several years, allow immigrants to feel comfortable with the language and culture. For many, this is the most difficult barrier to finding work and getting established in their new homeland.

Although services provided by community organizations, settlement agencies, and other sources help countless immigrants to North America, newcomers from the former Yugoslavia tend to rely more heavily on a network of family and friends to help them get started. Like other immigrants to North America, people from the former Yugoslavia are often drawn to areas having a large population of their respective ethnic group. Slovene immigrants tend to settle in Slovene communities, Macedonians in Macedonian communities, and so on. Many of these communities were established more than 100 years ago, when the immigrants came to North America in large numbers.

Slovene Communities

Ethnic Slovenes have been in North America since the early 1700s, but their first concentrated settlements were not established for another 150 years or more. In the middle and late 1800s, Slovene missionaries went to Ohio to convert American Indians and Europeans there to Catholicism. Journals published in Slovenia contained articles about the missionaries' exciting experiences, which in turn spurred more Slovenes to immigrate to North America and settle in Ohio in the late 1800s. During this time Slovene communities sprang up in cities such as Euclid, Barberton, Lorain, and Akron. Today significant numbers of ethnic Slovenes continue to live in these cities, but it is Cleveland that claims the largest Slovene population in North America. By the early 1900s, in fact, the only city in the world with more ethnic Slovene residents than Cleveland was Ljubljana, Slovenia's capital.

As more Slovene immigrants came to the United States for economic reasons, they expanded to Illinois, where they settled in Chicago, Joliet, LaSalle, and Springfield. Many headed east and created communities in industrial areas such as New York City; Bridgeport, Connecticut; and Pittsburgh, Bethlehem, Johnstown, and Canonsburg, Pennsylvania. New Slovene immigrants to the United States continue to be drawn to these communities.

Though the majority of Slovenes who come to North America settle in the United States, some make Canada their home. Slovene communities sprang up in Canada after the enactment of the U.S. Immigration Act of 1924, whose national-origin quotas severely restricted immigration from southern Europe. During this time, Slovene immigrants gravitated toward Ontario's cities, especially Toronto, Timmins, Hamilton, and St. Catherines, which still attract Slovenes today. Lake Country (British Columbia), and Winnipeg (Manitoba), were other popular destinations.

Today many Slovene immigrants to North America are entrepreneurs who want to open a small business, such as a grocery store, bakery, or meat market. For these people, settling in an established Slovene community makes good business sense, in addition to offering many social advantages. For example, where there is a large Slovene community, there will usually be a high demand for Slovene ethnic foods. And a shared language and cultural background frequently opens doors for immigrant entrepreneurs.

Croatian Communities

Most of today's Croatian communities in the United States
and Canada grew out of settlements that were first established
by immigrants seeking temporary employment in the late 1800s
and early 1900s. Many of these immigrants, particularly single
males, intended to stay in North America only for as long as it
took to make and save enough money to live comfortably in
Croatia. And while a proportion of these early immigrants did
return home, some put down roots in North America. Many
who came to work in the fishing industry, for example, settled
in the Pacific Northwest, the Delta region of Mississippi, and
various parts of British Columbia. Industrial areas, such as
Pennsylvania, Illinois, and Ontario, were also popular destinations for early Croatian immigrants. These communities, established more than a century ago, still attract newcomers today.
Currently in the United States, large groups of Croatians reside
in Chicago, New York City, Pittsburgh, Detroit, Cleveland,
Milwaukee, St. Paul, Minneapolis, Los Angeles, San Francisco,
and San Pedro, California.

Pittsburgh, Pennsylvania, is home to a large community of Slovenian Americans and a large community of Croatian Americans.

In Canada, small groups of immigrants also continue to migrate to areas where the earliest Croatian settlements were established. These include Ladner, Ladysmith, and Wellington in British Columbia; Lethbridge and Iron Springs in Alberta; and Transcona in Manitoba. However, the country's largest concentration of Croatians is in Ontario, in industrial areas such as Toronto, Hamilton, Welland, Sault Ste. Marie, and Port Arthur.

Many Croatians arrive in the United States or Canada without the prospect of employment. Some of these immigrants get information about job opportunities from periodicals such as the *Croatian America Times*, which is published weekly in the United States and Canada and is also available in Croatia. Others rely on family members and friends for contacts and job advice. Church functions, such as those held by Chicago's influential St. Jerome Croatian Catholic Church, also provide opportunities to network, as do cultural institutions like the Croatian Fraternal Union of America, located in Pittsburgh, and Vancouver's Croatian Cultural Center. In addition to their networking benefits, these religious and cultural institutions can create a sense of belonging, which is especially important for those who have few relatives and friends in the new country.

As with other immigrants to North America, job prospects for an individual Croatian hinge largely on his or her professional experience, education, and ability to speak the English language. Croatian immigrants have found work in fields ranging from engineering and medicine to food service and hotel management, the latter two being especially common because tourism is a pillar of Croatia's economy.

Macedonian Communities

During the late 1800s, Macedonian immigrants flocked to industrial areas in the United States and Canada in search of jobs. Some found work in road, railway, or canal construction; others worked as butchers, cooks, or dishwashers. As with early Croatian immigrants, many of these people intended their stay in North America to be temporary. But many never returned to the country of their birth, instead putting down roots in Canada or the United States. In many cases the tightly knit enclaves these Macedonian immigrants formed are today still home to their descendants, as well as to newly arrived Macedonian immigrant families.

Though they settled throughout the United States, Macedonians established particularly notable communities in Gary, Indiana; Detroit; Columbus, Cleveland, Canton, Massilon, and Cincinnati, all in Ohio; and New York City, Lackawanna, Buffalo, Rochester, and Syracuse in New York State. In Canada, Ontario was the province of choice, with communities in and around Toronto, Hamilton, Windsor, Mississauga, Markham, and Cambridge.

Important Macedonian cultural organizations include the United Macedonians and the Macedonian Patriotic Organization. Through the various educational, cultural, and academic programs these institutions sponsor, Macedonian immigrants can meet potential friends or employers. The organizations also provide scholarships and grants for the education of immigrant children.

Churches such as Sts. Peter and Paul Macedonian Orthodox Cathedral in Crown Point, Indiana, serve similar functions. At Mass and at social events sponsored by the church, newcomers have the chance to meet immigrants who are already established in the community.

Serbian and Montenegrin Communities

Serbs and Montenegrins are culturally and ethnically very similar; some people even insist that Montenegrins are indistinguishable from Serbs. For this reason, the two groups are constantly linked (despite the distinct histories of Serbia and Montenegro and a sense of national identity among many residents of the latter). What cannot be disputed, though, is that Serbs and Montenegrins have had strong, long-standing bonds—in the Balkans as well as in North American immigrant communities.

Serbian and Montenegrin immigrants first arrived in the United States in significant numbers during the late 1800s. As with other Balkan immigrants of the time, many planned to return to their homeland after working and saving enough money to live comfortably there. Large numbers did, in fact, return home—many of them to fight in the First and Second Balkan Wars and World War I. But many others remained in North America.

The first wave of Serbian and Montenegrin immigrants settled in California. But over the years, significant numbers headed east and established communities in Chicago, Pittsburgh, Detroit, and Cleveland. Others traveled north to Canada, where they settled in the towns of British Columbia, such as Fraser River and Vancouver. Serbian and Montenegrin communities in other Canadian provinces soon followed. Among the cities that hosted—and that continue to host—such communities were Lethbridge, Edmonton, and Calgary in Alberta; Regina in Saskatchewan; and Toronto, Hamilton, and Niagara Falls in Ontario.

Today many Serbs and Montenegrins who come to North America rely on family members already living in Canada or the United States to get settled. The relatives usually provide the immigrants with accommodations and job leads—often in the food service, trucking, or steel industries. They may also direct the newcomers to various business periodicals printed in their native language. Currently, there is no Montenegrin-language newspaper, but since Montenegrins use the same Cyrillic alphabet system as the Serbs, they can consult Serbian-language periodicals. *Nezavisne Novine*, published in Canada, provides a listing of Serbian businesses in the country and is read by Serbs and Montenegrins alike.

Serbs and Montenegrins, who are both predominantly Orthodox Christian, often attend the same churches. St. Sava Serbian Orthodox Cathedral in Cleveland and St. Stefan Orthodox Church in Ottawa have provided immigrants in need with housing, food, and clothing and have helped many newcomers find employment.

Cultural institutions also provide assistance and offer Serbian and Montenegrin immigrants the chance to socialize and network. Such organizations include the Montenegrin Association of America and the Ontario Centre for Newcomers (a division of the Serbian Heritage Academy).

Bosnian Communities

Before war erupted in the 1990s, relatively few people from Bosnia and Herzegovina immigrated to North America. Those who did were primarily ethnic Croats and Serbs. Members of these groups, known as Bosnian Croats and Bosnian Serbs, often moved to areas of the United States and Canada that had already been settled by immigrants from Croatia and Serbia. A smaller number of Bosnian Muslims, or Bosniacs, also made their way to North America. In the early 1900s, the destination of choice for Bosniacs was Chicago, an industrial city that offered them the prospect of employment.

The Bosnian presence in North America increased rapidly as a result of the civil war. In the decade following the war's outbreak in 1992, approximately 200,000 people from Bosnia and Herzegovina came to the United States and Canada as refugees. And even after the fighting had officially ended, the flow of refugees continued: as of 2001, Bosnia and Herzegovina was the leading source country for refugees admitted into the United States, with nearly 14,600 (twice the number admitted from the next-largest source country, Ukraine).

Various institutions and government agencies have worked to find housing for Bosnian refugees. In the United States, major resettlement sites include Chicago, Houston, Detroit, and Utica, New York. Other cities with substantial Bosnian refugee populations are Pittsburgh; Jacksonville, Florida; and St. Louis.

In Canada, meanwhile, resettlement agencies broker deals with real estate corporations to find affordable housing for the refugees in a variety of regions. The Bosnian newcomers have found housing in the cities of Toronto and Windsor in Ontario;

Lethbridge, Medicine Hat, and Calgary in Alberta; Moncton and Saint John in New Brunswick; Moose Jaw in Saskatchewan; and Vancouver in British Columbia. Once housing is secured, the resettlement agencies continue to work with the Bosnians through outreach programs that offer access to health care, English language classes, and, in some cases, job placement.

In 2001 refugees from Bosnia and Herzegovina accounted for more than 21 percent of the total number of refugees admitted into the United States.

Bosnian refugees frequently start out working in factories, food service companies, or maintenance positions. Many, however, have shown remarkable entrepreneurial spirit, accumulating savings and obtaining loans to open their own small businesses after just a few years in their new country.

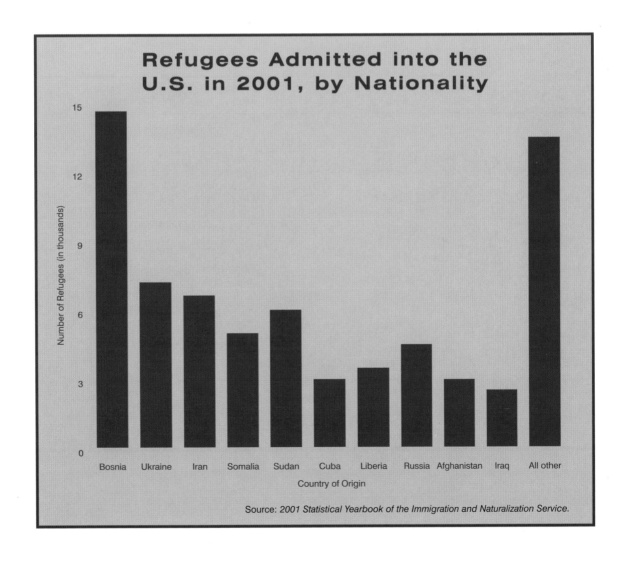

Refugees Admitted into the U.S. in 2001, by Nationality

Number of Refugees (in thousands)

Country of Origin

Source: *2001 Statistical Yearbook of the Immigration and Naturalization Service.*

5 OLD TRADITIONS MEET NEW LIFESTYLES

Immigrants come to North America for a variety of reasons: political and religious freedom, economic opportunity, a better life for themselves and their children. In order to fully enjoy these benefits and opportunities, most immigrants find it necessary to adopt—or at least adapt to—some of the customs, values, and practices in their new land. Yet at the same time, immigrants typically want to hold on to cherished aspects of their own culture, which may differ significantly from North American traditions. Immigrants from the former Yugoslavia are no exception. While they see the benefits of assimilation into mainstream American or Canadian society, Slovenes, Croats, Bosnians, Macedonians, Montenegrins, and Serbs are extremely proud of their heritage and want to preserve it in their new country.

Slovenes

Slovenes are, as a rule, devout Roman Catholics. Not surprisingly, many Slovene immigrants seek out churches specific to their ethnic background and prefer parishes that offer Mass in their native language. Many such parishes in North America are found in large Slovene communities. These include Saint Joseph in Joliet, Illinois; Saint Vitus in Cleveland; and Our Lady Help of Christians in Toronto. Slovene immigrants have always observed important Catholic holidays such as Easter, Christmas, Good Friday, and Lent.

◀ Catholicism is the predominant religion in Slovenia and Croatia, and the Catholic Church continues to play an important role in the lives of Slovene and Croat immigrants in North America.

In Slovenia, a great deal of emphasis is placed on Lent. The 40 days of this religious holiday are often kicked off with a huge carnival. This is perhaps the greatest spectacle in Slovenia. Much like Mardi Gras in New Orleans, or Carnival in Venice and Rio de Janeiro, the "Pust" in Slovenia is filled with a grand display of singing and dancing. Polka bands are a popular attraction during this event. Common foods at the festival include doughnuts and *potica*—a sweet walnut roll that is also eaten at Christmas and Easter. Many Pust participants wear elaborate masks and costumes. The most popular of these is that of the *kurent*, a mythical Slovene figure; the costume consists of layers of sheepskin with a cowbell dangling from the waist, a furry hat, and a dark leather mask with a long, red tongue.

In North America, there are no such Slovene carnivals. Immigrants and their descendants may instead enjoy a banquet or dance sponsored by churches or cultural institutions such as the Canadian Slovenian Cultural Society, the American Slovenian Catholic Union, or the Slovenian Heritage Center. Pust banquets are usually held in great halls known as "national homes." These national homes exist in Slovene communities throughout North America for the purpose of holding meetings, cultural events, and parties.

Polka groups are often invited to play at banquets and dances. With its characteristic accordions and button boxes, polka music is part of all Slavic culture. But among the peoples of the former Yugoslavia, it is most popular with Slovenes. Polka musicians are often accompanied by dancers dressed in traditional costumes. These costumes may include a white shirt, vest, and wide-brimmed hat for the men, and a white headdress and colorful dress with tassels for the women.

Many Slovenes living in North America are able to keep track of Pust banquets and other cultural events with the help of periodicals, ethnic radio stations, and the Internet. Ethnic periodicals, such as *Vecer* and *Republika*, are available in Slovene national homes. Such publications also keep immigrants abreast

The making of bobbin lace is a traditional pastime that many ethnic Slovenes in the United States and Canada continue to practice.

of developments in their homeland, though many also rely on friends and family members in Slovenia for such news.

One important craft tradition that Slovene immigrants to North America have maintained is the art of lace making. Bobbin lace, an intricate lace made by interlacing thread around small, notched pins stuck into a pillow, has been a part of Slovene heritage since the 17th century. But bobbin lace first became a commercially significant product after technological advances put miners out of work in the town of Idrija. As a way to replace the lost income, residents of Idrija began making lace, and the practice gradually spread to other regions of Slovenia. In 1876 the first lace-making school opened in Idrija; other schools soon followed. In time, thousands of Slovenians were able to learn the craft. Lace making became such a popular pastime that many immigrants carried the tradition with them in their travels. Since the making of bobbin lace does not require workshops or complicated tools, immigrants who practice this craft find it easy to maintain abroad.

Croatians

Unlike many earlier Croatian groups who immigrated to North America with low literacy levels and little or no understanding of the English language, the recent pool of immigrants has, on the whole, been younger and more educated. Many are proficient in English, having studied it in school, and many have occupational skills that allow them to establish themselves in

A couple, dressed in traditional costume, perform a Croatian folk dance. The musician at the left of the photo is playing a *tamburitza*.

the North American workforce. This new wave of immigrants has included professors, scientists, artists, doctors, and engineers. These immigrants easily assimilate into American and Canadian society, but without losing a sense of their homeland.

Since the republic declared itself an independent nation in 1991, Croatians everywhere have been more determined than ever to preserve their national identity. Like other immigrant groups from the former Yugoslavia, Croatians have been able to do so with the help of various cultural institutions. The Croatian Academy of America is a cultural organization with chapters throughout North America. The academy educates its members and the general public about Croatian history and culture by sponsoring lectures and publishing the *Journal of Croatian Studies*. Another important institution is the Croatian Fraternal Union. Established in 1894, it is the oldest Croatian cultural organization in North America. At its headquarters in Pittsburgh is a Croatian museum that houses works by artists such as Ivan Lackovic-Croata and Ivan Mestrovic.

At the root of Croatian folkloric music is the *tamburitza*, a stringed instrument similar to the mandolin, which has been in the Balkan region since the 14th century. To many Croatians living outside Croatia, the tamburitza is a cultural symbol that binds them to their homeland. Learning to play this instrument has been a tradition passed down from generation to generation. Most villages in Croatia have their share of tamburitza players who perform for every festive occasion. In North America, this tradition continues. Many Croatian immigrants, as well as those descended from immigrants, continue to take tamburitza lessons in various schools and cultural centers. As a result, the United States and Canada have their own tamburitza groups, which perform in ethnic festivals in North America and occasionally tour Croatia as well.

The tamburitza musicians are often accompanied by folk dance groups. Much like tamburitza music, folk dancing has attracted a large following among Croatian Americans and Canadians, many of whom take lessons to learn it and attend festivals to see it performed.

About three-quarters of all Croatian citizens practice the Roman Catholic faith, and the church continues to play an important role in the lives of Croat immigrants in North America. Croats, like Slovenes, observe the traditional Catholic holidays, but with a few distinct touches. On Holy Saturday, Catholic Croats may take foods such as smoked pork, bread, and boiled eggs to church to have them blessed. A small portion of the food is left at church as a token of thanks. The blessed food is then eaten with a traditional feast on Easter Sunday.

In Croatia, the traditional Easter meal usually includes roasted lamb and sweet Easter bread. Children may eat dyed eggs and expect gifts from the Easter bunny. These traditions are still practiced in North America, but one thing has changed. In Croatia (as well as Slovenia), Easter is a two-day holiday. Though most of the festivities are practiced on Sunday, many families will also gather on Easter Monday. In the United States and Canada, some parishes do offer a special Mass on this day, but the festivities are generally limited to Sunday.

Christmas and the holy days leading up to it are also filled with many unique customs. Though Croats exchange some presents on Christmas, the majority of gifts are given on St. Nicholas Day (December 6). In some regions in Croatia, gifts are given on St. Lucy's Day (December 13). Many Croatian families in North America uphold these practices, though most exchange the majority of gifts on Christmas.

Food plays a major part during a traditional Croatian Christmas. In honor of the occasion, a bread called *Badnji Kruh* is baked. The bread dough is made with nutmeg, raisins, and almonds, braided into a wreath and glazed. Many Croats place wheat and candles in the center of the wreath and use it as a table centerpiece. *Licitar* hearts are another common Christmas tradition. These heart-shaped cookies, made of red-colored dough and decorated with sparkling sugars, are used as tree ornaments. An assortment of candies in brightly colored wrappers are also used to adorn Christmas trees. Many Croatian immigrants continue to practice these customs, though they often modify them when the required ingredients are unavailable.

Bosnians

Recent arrivals to North America from Bosnia and Herzegovina—particularly Bosnian Muslim refugees—seem determined to preserve their culture. They have established various cultural organizations to help them in this quest. For example, the Bosnia and Herzegovina Community Center in Chicago and the BC Bosnian Association in Vancouver commemorate national Bosnian holidays such as Statehood Day and Independence Day with picnics and other celebrations. The Slavic Cultural Organization in San Francisco, among other groups, organizes dance performances and exhibits Bosnian artwork, such as fine metalwork, silk embroidery, and hand-woven rugs, which were once a common wedding gift. Bosnian youth organizations also keep the culture of their homeland alive. Many high

A Bosnian carpet trader displays his wares at a Sarajevo market. The making of hand-woven rugs, which traditionally were given as wedding presents, is an important part of Bosnian culture.

schools in Bosnian-populated areas have clubs where students perform traditional poetry, music, and dance. These high school clubs also provide a place for Bosnian students to meet and share their war-related experiences.

Folk festivals that take place throughout the year highlight various aspects of Bosnian culture, especially music. Bosnian music, which has a strong Turkish influence, can be divided into two styles—the rural and the urban. The rural style includes both flat, monotone songs and lively, multi-tone harmonies that are usually accompanied by a long-necked lute called a *sargija*, a wooden flute, or a type of bagpipe called a *diple*. In the urban style of music, more than one note per syllable must be played. This is usually characterized by the sound of an elaborate lute, called a *saz*.

Traditional dance groups are another attraction at Bosnian folk festivals. These groups entertain the crowds with a variety of dances, the most common being the *kolo*. In Bosnia the kolo is not performed to music, but rather only to the beat of stomping feet. This "silent" dance has a leader who gives verbal or physical cues to instruct the other dancers on how quickly and in what pattern they should move. Traditional dance is extremely popular among Bosnians, and many immigrants have their children take lessons to learn it.

The homes of Bosnian families are as distinctive as the people themselves. In a traditional Bosnian home, the furniture in the living area is positioned in a U-shaped arrangement with a large, low table in the center. This is an important area where families and friends socialize. While entertaining, many Bosnian immigrants continue to serve traditional dishes such as *cevapcici*, which are small sausages made from ground meat and spices; *dolmas*, grape leaves filled with a mixture of rice, meat, and spices; and coffee served from a small cup called a *findzan*.

Until the war, Bosnia—Yugoslavia's most ethnically balanced republic—had been a place where Eastern and Western influences, including religion, mixed and were shared. Four major religions—Catholicism, Eastern Orthodoxy, Islam, and Judaism—existed within the republic's boundaries. Religious holidays became social affairs, with believers of all faiths taking part in one another's festivities. Catholics would visit Muslim households during Kurban Bajram (a holiday commemorating the willingness of the prophet Abraham to sacrifice his son to Allah, or God), and Muslims would attend Christmas services with Eastern Orthodox friends. Many refugees—especially those in interfaith marriages—continue to observe holidays in this manner. But others, particularly Muslims who were prohibited from practicing certain religious traditions, have become stricter about their beliefs.

Macedonians

Like other immigrant groups from the former Yugoslavia, Macedonians in North America rely on a variety of organizations and institutions to keep their culture alive. Publications such as *Ilinden's Monthly* help keep Macedonian immigrants and their children connected to their language and literature. Organizations like the United Macedonians, the Macedonian Cultural Center Ilinden, and the Selyani Folklore Group in Toronto work with groups in Macedonia and North America to establish cultural programs in schools, clubs, and churches where immigrants are present in large numbers. The programs often revolve around Macedonian arts—including folk music, dance, and embroidery—and the history behind them. Macedonian cultural institutions also sponsor social functions, such as picnics, dinners, and dances.

Folk ensembles consisting of dancers and orchestras are staples at these cultural functions. The orchestras play lively folk music using instruments characteristic of their home region. These include violins, clarinets, and accordions, as well as more traditional Macedonian instruments such as the *gaida*, the *kaval*, the *tambura*, and the *tapan*. The dancers, dressed in traditional Macedonian attire, entertain crowds with variations of the kolo. Though many of these troupes come directly from

Macedonia, some Macedonians living in North America also take classes to learn and maintain this great tradition. Folk ensembles often perform at weddings and in church halls during holidays and ethnic festivals. The folk ensembles are also common at the Sunday evening parties organized by many Macedonian churches.

The Macedonian Orthodox Church in North America plays an important role in maintaining tradition, although some religious customs have been modified to blend better with North American practices. Weddings are a good example. During a traditional Orthodox ceremony in Macedonia, the priest ties the hands of the bride and groom together as a symbol of unity, then places crowns on their heads to symbolize the glory that is being bestowed on the marriage. In North America, Macedonian wedding ceremonies uphold these traditions, but the similarities generally stop there. In Macedonia, the bride and groom would wear special wedding costumes characterized by lavish embroidery. In the United States and Canada, a white gown with veil is a more common choice for the bride, while the groom, like most American and Canadian men, sports a

The Cyrillic Alphabet

The Cyrillic alphabet, used in Serbia and Montenegro (as well as in other Slavic countries such as Russia and Bulgaria), is named after St. Cyril, a ninth-century Byzantine missionary. Cyril, who made it his life's work to convert the Slavs to Christianity, is said to have invented the script so that he could translate the Bible into Slavic.

In recent times, however, the Cyrillic alphabet has gradually been losing ground to the Roman alphabet in the former Yugoslav republics. But many immigrants, intent on saving Cyrillic, send their children to special language schools in the United States and Canada, where they can learn the Yugoslav version of the Cyrillic alphabet. The following are examples of Cyrillic letters, along with their Roman equivalents:

Ф – F   И – I   Л – L

tuxedo. Social traditions have also changed. Gone is the procession from the ceremony to the reception. In Macedonia, the bride and groom walk to the reception while accompanied by their guests and a band. With its limit of small streets and its abundance of traffic lights, North America is not conducive to such a practice. Here, a wedding procession would only lead to congestion.

The Macedonian Church also ensures that immigrants in North America continue to observe religious holidays as they did in their home country. In addition to more traditional holidays such as Christmas (observed on January 7) and Easter, Macedonians observe *Slava*, a special day set aside to honor their family protector saint. On this day, different families practice different traditions, but the most common revolves around Mass. At this service, a family observing its Slava presents a *poskura* (a patron saint cake) and a bowl of cooked wheat sweetened with sugar or honey to a priest to bless. During the liturgy, the priest will also read aloud a list of the family's deceased relatives. When the ceremony is over, the family returns home to eat the poskura and cooked wheat.

Macedonian immigrants also continue to celebrate *Imenden*, or Name Day. Most Macedonian names are derived from the names of saints. Each person honors his or her saint on a day especially set aside for this purpose. The celebrations often involve a simple gathering of family and friends. Imenden days occur throughout the year.

Serbs and Montenegrins

Approximately 65 percent of Serbs and Montenegrins are Orthodox Christians. They celebrate traditional Christian holidays with church services, but they also have some unique customs. On Christmas Eve (celebrated on January 6), it is customary to stand before one's house and fire a weapon into the sky to announce the birth of Christ. Surprisingly, this custom is still practiced in large Serbian and Montenegrin communities in North America, such as Jackson, California.

In addition to Christmas and other traditional religious holidays such as Easter and Palm Sunday, Serbs and Montenegrins celebrate the Feast of St. Sava, on January 27. St. Sava, the patron saint of education, is Serbia and Montenegro's most important saint. Students and teachers spend much class time reflecting on the importance of this religious figure and often put on performances that honor the saint's life. This practice does not continue in North America, where immigrant students are generally enrolled in schools attended by a multicultural student population. However, this special day is acknowledged by the Serbian Orthodox Church, often with banquets that follow performances by children.

Serbs and Montenegrins, like Macedonians, are named after saints. And traditionally the Slava—which is celebrated on the saint's feast day—is more important than a birthday celebration.

Chicago has a large and well-established community of Serbs and Montenegrins.

A Slava celebration involves praying to the saint, then feasting on a special loaf-bread called *Slavski Kolac*, which has been blessed by a priest. It is also customary for families and even social institutions to have patron saints.

Serbs and Montenegrins have a rich tradition of folk music, which is still appreciated by their immigrant communities in North America. Serbian music is characterized by four instrument groups: aerophones, or instruments that use air to produce sound, including the flute-like *frula* and *klanet*; chordophones, or stringed instruments such as the violin; membraphones, or percussion instruments such as the drum; and idiophones, instruments that are plucked or rattled and don't need to be tuned, including a harp called the *drombulje*. Songs performed to the sound of these instruments were originally work songs for peasants or shepherds. The rhythms of the different songs often reflect the rhythms of the work that was being done, like plowing, picking, or mowing.

Folk dances performed to this music—such as the ever-popular kolo—differ in rhythm, in step, and in the direction dancers move. These qualities are all dictated by the nature of the dance. A celebratory dance calls for lively, quick steps, while a dance to honor the dead is characterized by the movement of dancers in a counterclockwise direction. The tradition of this dancing and music is upheld by folk ensembles that entertain immigrant crowds during festivals, and by cultural schools that offer instruction in these arts.

6 OBSTACLES TO OVERCOME

Immigrants face a variety of challenges as they attempt to make new lives for themselves and their families. Immediate concerns include finding a place to live and getting a job. Obtaining health care is frequently an issue as well. And, for many immigrants, particularly adults, learning a new language can be especially difficult.

Housing

When they immigrate to North America, people from the former Yugoslavia, like newcomers from other countries, tend to gravitate toward areas where members of their family or friends have already settled. It is not uncommon for new arrivals to live with members of their extended family, or with friends, as they get established.

But for immigrants who cannot rely on the help of family and friends, housing can be a major concern. Finding good, affordable housing can be very difficult, especially in the large cities of the United States and Canada, where vacancies are frequently scarce and rents high. Many immigrants end up living in crowded units located in less desirable neighborhoods. According to the 1999 National Survey of America's Families, nearly 30 percent of immigrant children live in housing where there are more than two people per bedroom. A study by Canada's Supporting Communities Partnership Initiative found that the dwellings inhabited by many immigrants "do not meet

◀ The underdeveloped economy of much of the former Yugoslavia has left many immigrants from the region—particularly older ones—ill prepared for the demands of the North American labor market. Here a woman does embroidery on a street in Dubrovnik, Croatia.

basic maintenance standards, neither regarding the cleanliness of the unit itself, nor the structural state of the entire property." Many immigrants who live in such units find that their complaints of drafts, leaks, and insufficient heat during the winter go unheeded by landlords.

Job Search

Finding a job in North America can be extremely challenging for newly arrived immigrants from the former Yugoslavia. One reason is that the immigrants are unaccustomed to job-hunting rules in Canada and the United States. In the republics of the former Yugoslavia, most employees are hired based solely on the credentials listed in their job applications. In the United States and Canada, a job interview is nearly always required. For many immigrants unfamiliar with this process, interviewing can be a nerve-wracking experience. Plus, for people whose English-language skills are less than perfect, writing the obligatory résumés, cover letters, and thank-you notes can be a major obstacle.

And job hunting can be difficult for immigrant professionals as well as blue-collar workers. People who were engineers, architects, lawyers, or physicians in the former Yugoslavia find they must apply for certification to practice their chosen career in the United States or Canada. Many are told they must take some additional courses to meet U.S. and Canadian licensing standards or, even worse, that their education and experience are simply not transferable. According to a study conducted by the Vancouver Centre for Excellence, many former Yugoslavians believe that their "exclusion from the labor market is a systematic effort to reserve better job opportunities for native-born citizens." In any event, the additional requirements can set immigrants back professionally by several years. This wait is sometimes too much to handle, and in the end many immigrants wind up changing careers or accepting lower-level positions. This is especially true of those in the medical and legal professions.

Language

The English language has increasingly become a staple in the school curricula of countries such as Croatia and Slovenia. However, this is a relatively recent development. Thus, with the exception of those who are very well educated or employees in the tourist industry, most older immigrants from the former Yugoslavia have minimal English-language skills. This is especially true of refugees, who move to the new region abruptly and have virtually no time to prepare with English classes.

Both the United States and Canada offer language classes aimed at immigrants. Canada's LINC program is free to all qualified immigrants. In the United States, immigrants generally must pay a fee when they take ESL classes at a community college or other outlet for adult education. Though ESL classes have proven effective in teaching not just the English language, but also customs and etiquette in the United States, not all immigrants are able to enroll. Many newcomers work multiple jobs and simply do not have the time to devote to learning. Others do not live in areas where the special classes are offered. Still others, struggling to pay for housing and food, cannot afford the ESL classes—even at the inexpensive cost at which they are typically offered. Immigrants who are unable to speak English are at a disadvantage in the job market.

Health Care Services

Under the best of circumstances, immigrating to a new land—a course of action rife with challenges and uncertainties—can be an emotionally trying experience. For many refugees from the former Yugoslavia, especially Bosnians and Kosovars, the traumatic events that brought them to North America constitute a formidable barrier to adjustment. Many of these refugees saw their homes and villages destroyed, or loved ones killed before their very eyes. Many were beaten or raped; some lived in concentration camps reminiscent of the World War II variety. The mental and emotional stress created

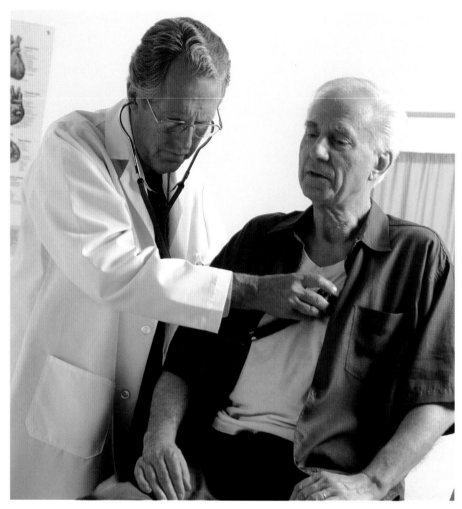

Obtaining health care can be a major issue for immigrants. In Canada government-sponsored medical coverage is available after a newcomer has been granted permanent resident status, but that process is often lengthy. In the United States, low-income refugees may receive Medicaid, but immigrants are generally ineligible for federal benefits until they have been in the country for five years.

by such horrible experiences can cause lingering problems, including sleep and eating disorders and difficulties concentrating or even remembering simple things. For many such deeply affected refugees, the difficulties of learning a new language or finding a job are only magnified. Some may require health services that include personal counseling.

In the United States, the cost of medical services is usually the individual's responsibility. However, refugees with low incomes are eligible to receive Medicaid, which pays for health insurance for lower-income U.S. residents. Immigrants more generally are ineligible for federal benefits unless they have been in the country for at least five years.

In Canada, refugees are not eligible to receive government-sponsored health coverage. They must become permanent residents first—a process that involves a good deal of paperwork and a lot of time. As they wait for their permanent resident claims to be processed, they are offered Interim Federal Health, a policy that covers the expense of urgent and essential medical services. This policy, though, is only offered for a brief period and rarely covers the duration of the refugees' permanent resident application process. Once permanent resident status is approved, a person may apply for a health insurance card, which gives him or her access to medical services at the government's expense.

7 AN UNCERTAIN
FUTURE

Since 1965, when the United States ended its national-origin immigration quotas and Yugoslavia relaxed its closed-border policy, tens of thousands of people from the republics of Slovenia, Croatia, Bosnia and Herzegovina, Macedonia, Serbia, and Montenegro have moved to North America. For the first two and a half decades after these changes, economic considerations played a primary role in decisions to immigrate. But beginning in 1991, when civil war erupted, many left to escape the terrible ethnic violence. A dozen years later, the wars are over and the Federal Republic of Yugoslavia is gone, replaced by four independent republics and the loosely affiliated Serbia and Montenegro. The future of emigration from the region will most likely vary considerably, depending on economic and political conditions in the individual republics.

Slovenia: A Success Story

The most prosperous republic of the former Yugoslavia, Slovenia had a relatively easy time making the transition to independence. Today it enjoys a stable, democratic government and a prosperous economy. In 2002 its gross domestic product (GDP) per capita—a measure of each citizen's average share of the wealth the country creates annually—was estimated at $18,000. That's on par with the GDP per capita of Portugal. Furthermore, Slovenia's population enjoys a developing system

◄ After years of violence, the now-independent republics of the former Yugoslavia continue to confront the difficult task of rebuilding—physically, socially, and economically. And the future political stability of the region is by no means guaranteed.

of benefits, including mandatory health insurance. In addition, in the spring of 2003, Slovenians voted in a national referendum to accept membership in the European Union (EU). This development would allow for increased trade with other nations in the EU, and thus further benefit Slovenia's economy.

With such favorable prospects, it's unlikely that a large number of Slovenians will choose to emigrate, and fewer still will head for North America. Indeed, the United States reported only 76 Croatian immigrants in the year 2000, and that number may not grow in the upcoming years.

Croatia: Progress Amid Setbacks

Compared with Slovenia, Croatia has experienced greater economic, political, and social difficulties in the years since gaining independence. The country's once strong economy declined after Croatia seceded from Yugoslavia, and at least part of the blame must go to the policies of former president Franjo Tudjman, who ruled until his death in 1999. Tudjman rewarded political supporters by giving them control of various businesses, which in many cases they ran inefficiently and corruptly. Furthermore, Tudjman's strong sense of nationalism—and his promotion of ethnic cleansing within Croatia's borders—alienated many Western countries that could have aided his country during its transition. As trade and tourism declined, thousands of jobs were lost. By 2002 the GDP per capita stood at an estimated $8,800—less than half the income Slovenians enjoyed.

In 2000 a new Croatian government led by President Stjepan Mesic and Prime Minister Ivica Racan sought to repair Croatia's image within the world community by cooperating with war crimes investigations. The government hoped that this would pay economic dividends by creating a more favorable climate for foreign investment and trade, part of an overall strategy for economic restructuring. But significant problems remain. In 2002 unemployment was estimated at a whopping 20 percent. High-level jobs for the educated are particularly difficult to come by, and wages for those positions are comparatively low.

As a result, a significant number of Croatians, especially among the well-educated younger generation, continue to emigrate for employment reasons. The countries of choice, though, are in Europe—not North America. Germany and neighboring Slovenia are popular destinations, but Austria leads the way. In 1999 more than 23,000 Croatians immigrated to Austria.

More than 2,800 Croatian immigrants were admitted into the United States in 2001, according to the Immigration and Naturalization Service. In addition, several hundred people from Croatia have been accepted annually as refugees by the United States. In 2002 the figure stood at 305.

Macedonia: Continuing Poverty

Macedonia is a poor nation beset by high unemployment (an estimated 35 percent in 2002). Yet relatively few Macedonians have immigrated to North America. In 2001 the number reached 924 in the United States, the highest total since the U.S. government recognized Macedonia's independence in 1994. In that year immigration officials recorded 367 Macedonian newcomers. In Canada, meanwhile, a high of 218 Macedonian immigrants gained entry in 1994.

During the 1990s, Macedonia escaped the ethnic violence that tore through much of Yugoslavia. But in 2001 long-simmering tensions between the Macedonian majority (about 66 percent of the population) and the country's large ethnic Albanian minority (about 23 percent) erupted into fighting. Ethnic Albanian rebels and Macedonian security forces battled for several months before signing a peace treaty in August. By the terms of the agreement, the number of Albanians in the Macedonian police force was increased; the Albanian language became permitted in official institutions such as the country's parliament, where a large number of ethnic Albanians served; and the preamble of the nation's constitution was rewritten to upgrade the status of the Albanians and other ethnic minorities.

During the unrest, about 175,000 citizens were displaced. Many sought refuge in Europe. By 2002, however, about 131,500 had returned home. But the return of the refugees did little to help Macedonia's economic prospects. On the contrary, it only increased the country's already high unemployment rate. For the young and well educated, emigration is an option. Many have moved to Europe, especially Austria. Relatively few have looked to North America, though continuing economic difficulties in Macedonia may change that in the coming years.

Picking Up the Pieces: Bosnia and Herzegovina

The Dayton Accords, signed in December 1995, ended Bosnia and Herzegovina's civil war. The agreement kept the country's external borders intact but created two internal political divisions: the Bosniac-Croat Federation and the Serb-controlled Republika Srpska.

Since that time, political and social conditions have improved dramatically. The Office of High Administration (OHR), a civilian agency created by the Dayton Accords and composed of international and local officials, has the power to impose

Vojislav Kostunica greets well-wishers before taking the oath of office as Yugoslavia's president, October 7, 2000.

legislation and keep nationalism in check. In addition, a contingent of NATO peacekeeping troops, known as SFOR (for "stabilization force"), remains in the country to prevent future outbreaks of violence. By the end of 2002, there were about 12,000 SFOR soldiers in Bosnia and Herzegovina.

Because of the improved political situation, fewer Bosnians are leaving the country, and many who left during the war have returned. Nevertheless, ethnic tensions remain, and isolated outbreaks of violence occur with some regularity. Moreover, the country's economy is troubled: in 2002, unemployment was estimated at 40 percent, and GDP per capita stood at around $1,800.

For these reasons, emigration from Bosnia has continued at high levels. In 2001 more than 23,600 Bosnians entered the United States as immigrants. They were joined by nearly 14,600 countrymen and women admitted as refugees. By the following year, though, the U.S. Department of State took steps to reduce the number of Bosnian refugees coming to the United States, proposing a 9,000-person ceiling for refugees from the former Yugoslavia (down from the 16,500-person ceiling imposed the previous year). The year 2004 may mark the end of large-scale Bosnian refugee admissions into the United States. Meanwhile, Canada's long and extensive admission process, which involves evaluating a refugee's ability to resettle in the country, makes the United States' northern neighbor an even less likely destination for Bosnian refugees.

Ruins of a Nation: Serbia and Montenegro

The pursuit of a "Greater Serbia"—the dream of Slobodan Milosevic and his political allies and followers—led only to the violent dissolution of Yugoslavia. Although Milosevic was replaced in 2000 by a popularly elected president, Vojislav Kostunica, and although he was later arrested and put on trial in The Hague for war crimes, Serbia and Montenegro continue to suffer under the legacy of his rule. Ethnic warfare, international economic sanctions, and NATO bombing devastated the republics' economies and infrastructures. Three of every 10 residents of Serbia and Montenegro were living in poverty by 2002; an equal proportion of workers were unemployed. With average monthly wages at just $40 and inflation running at about 18 percent, even those fortunate enough to hold a job were likely to have trouble affording overpriced basic necessities such as oil, sugar, and bread.

Such difficult conditions have prompted many to seek work abroad, but the large expense associated with moving has proved to be a formidable obstacle—in the depressed economy, even selling one's house to generate money can be difficult. In part because of the higher costs of moving to North America, the vast majority of Serbian and Montenegrin immigrants set their sights on neighboring European countries. Germany, Switzerland, Austria, and Sweden all experienced large influxes of Serbian and Montenegrin workers in 2001.

Long-term immigration patterns are uncertain, as they are closely linked to the economic and political future of Serbia and Montenegro. The government has been working hard to promote the privatization of businesses and to attract investment. In addition, with Milosevic no longer in power and foreign relations much improved, many people see reasons for optimism about the future. But the assassination of Serbian prime minister Zoran Djindjic on March 12, 2003, put a damper on that optimism. The killing, thought to be the work of organized-crime groups acting in concert with elements of the Serbian security forces, had many citizens fearing a renewal of political violence.

A Secondary Destination

Over the past 30 years, the United States and Canada have welcomed comparatively few immigrants from the former Yugoslavia. Such countries and regions as Mexico, the Philippines, and Central America, for example, have sent far more people to North America. It's likely that this trend will

A crowd pays tribute to Serbia's fallen prime minister, Zoran Djindjic, who was assassinated on March 12, 2003. The killing, thought to be the work of organized crime groups and members of the Serbian security forces, raised fears of renewed violence in Serbia.

continue. For would-be immigrants from Slovenia, Croatia, Bosnia and Herzegovina, Macedonia, Serbia, and Montenegro, nearby Europe will probably remain a more attractive destination than either Canada or the United States. Of the approximately 800,000 to one million legal immigrants that the United States accepts each year, and of the 200,000 to 250,000 that Canada takes in, only a small fraction can be expected to hail from the former Yugoslavia.

Famous Immigrants from the Former Yugoslavia

Vlade Divac. Serbian-born basketball player Vlade Divac was one of the first non-Americans to star in the NBA. A 7'1" center, Divac has played for the Los Angeles Lakers, Charlotte Hornets, and Sacramento Kings.

Milan Panic. Born in Belgrade, Serbia, businessman Milan Panic immigrated to the United States in 1956. In 1960 he launched the International Chemical and Nuclear Corporation (ICN)—a company that produces biomedical products. In 1992 Panic temporarily stepped down from his post as chief executive officer of ICN to serve as prime minister of Yugoslavia.

Tomaz Salamun. This famed Slovene poet was born in Zagreb, Croatia, in 1941, but grew up in Koper, Slovenia. He burst onto the literary scene in 1966 with the publication of *Poker*, and he has since published more than 20 poetry collections. Salamun now resides in New York City.

Monica Seles. Born in 1973 in Novi Sad, Vojvodina, now a semi-autonomous province within Serbia, tennis star Monica Seles moved to the United States in 1985. By 1991 she was the top-ranked female tennis player in the world, a position she held for 178 consecutive weeks.

Charles Simic. Born in Belgrade in 1938, this world-renowned poet and translator came to the United States at the age of 15. Simic attended New York University and published his first full-length collection of poems, *What the Grass Says*, a year after graduating. Since then, he has written more than 60 poetry collections, including the Pulitzer Prize–winning *The World Doesn't End: Prose Poems*, published in 1990.

Steve Stavro. Born in the village of Gabresh in Macedonia, businessman Steve Stavro immigrated to Toronto, Canada, as a young boy. Under his direction, Knob Hill Farms became Canada's largest independently owned food retailer. Stavro has also been a part owner of the National Hockey League Toronto Maple Leafs and an owner of the National Basketball Association Toronto Raptors.

Goran Visnjic. Born in the coastal town of Sibenik in Croatia, actor Goran Visnjic appeared in numerous Croatian plays before landing a role in *Welcome to Sarajevo*, an English-language film in which he won acclaim for his portrayal of a Bosnian interpreter during the civil war. In 1999 he joined the cast of NBC's top-rated television series, *ER*. Visnjic now lives in Los Angeles.

GLOSSARY

annexation: the taking and incorporation of territory into a larger state.

assimilation: the process by which a minority group becomes integrated into mainstream society.

autonomous: having the right or power of self-government.

communism: a political and social system characterized by state ownership of the means of production, state control of the distribution of goods, and one-party political rule.

embargo: an official order by a government that prohibits trade or commercial activity with another country.

emigration: the act of leaving one's country to live in another.

enterprise: a commercial undertaking or venture, such as a startup business.

ethnic cleansing: the expulsion, imprisonment, or killing of people belonging to a particular ethnic group as a means of solidifying control of an area (usually by a majority group).

immigration: the act of moving to and settling in another country.

nationalism: the belief that the independence, interests, and culture of one's own nation should take precedence over the rights and interests of other nations or groups.

oppression: persecution; the subjecting of individuals or groups to harsh and unfair treatment.

permanent resident: any person who is living in a particular country after being legally admitted as an immigrant, but who is not a citizen of that country.

refugee: a person who flees his or her home country in order to escape oppression, persecution, or war.

resettlement: the permanent relocation of refugees in a place outside their country of origin.

sanctions: a punitive measure or group of measures (for example, trade restrictions) adopted by several countries in order to coerce a nation to stop a particular course of action deemed to be in violation of international law.

transition: a movement, development, or evolution from one form, stage, or style to another.

Further Reading

Bauder, Harald, and Emilie Cameron. *Research on Immigration and Integration in the Metropolis* (No. 02-03). Vancouver: Vancouver Centre of Excellence, 2002.

Blumenthal, Shirley. *Coming to America: Immigrants from Eastern Europe*. New York: Delacorte Press, 1981.

Capps, Randy. *Hardship Among Children of Immigrants: Findings from the 1999 National Survey of America's Families* (Series B, No. B-29). Washington, D.C.: The Urban Institute, February 2001.

George, Usha. *The Settlement and Adaptation of Former-Yugoslavian Newcomers*. Toronto: Centre for Applied Social Research, 1997.

Kosinski, Leszek *A. Yugoslavs in Canada.* Edmonton, Alberta: Division of East European Studies, University of Alberta, 1980.

Little, Allan, and Laura Silber. *Yugoslavia: Death of a Nation.* New York: Penguin Books, 1997.

Oliver, Jeanne. *Croatia*. Victoria, Australia: Lonely Planet Publications, 2002.

Schierup, Carl-Ulrik. *Migration, Socialism, and the Division of Labour*. Hants, England: Averbury, 1990.

Wight, Ellen. *Bosnians in Chicago: Transnational Activities and Obstacles to Transnationalism.* Brighton, UK: Sussex Centre for Migration Research, 2000.

Zimmerman, William. *Open Borders, Non Alignment, and the Political Evolution of Yugoslavia*. Princeton, N.J.: Princeton University Press, 1987.

INTERNET RESOURCES

http://www.alertnet.org/thefacts/countryprofiles/

Brief facts pertaining to population, geography, and society in all the former Yugoslav republics, as well as up-to-date news.

http://www.croatiaemb.org/

The official website of the Embassy of the Republic of Croatia to the United States of America provides key information about the history and current status of Croatia.

http://www.bhembassy.org/

The official website of the Embassy of Bosnia and Herzegovina to the United States of America offers key information about Bosnia and Herzegovina as well as many links to related sites.

http://www.countrywatch.com/cw_country.asp?vcountry=104

This website features a country map and key information about Macedonia, along with links to political and economic sites that pertain to the republic.

http://www.embassy.org/slovenia

The official website of the Embassy of the Republic of Slovenia to the United States provides general information about the embassy and offers links to sites pertaining to Slovenia.

http://www.yuembusa.org/

The official website of the Embassy of Serbia and Montenegro provides economic information and links to news sites.

http://www.state.gov/g/prm/

Website for the U.S. Department of State's Bureau of Population, Refugees, and Migration.

http://www.uscr.org/

Website of the U.S. Committee for Refugees.

INDEX

Numbers in ***bold italic*** refer to captions.

Index

CONTRIBUTORS

SENATOR EDWARD M. KENNEDY has represented Massachusetts in the United States Senate for more than 40 years. Kennedy serves on the Senate Judiciary Committee, where he is the senior Democrat on the Immigration Subcommittee. He currently is the ranking member on the Health, Education, Labor and Pensions Committee in the Senate, and also serves on the Armed Services Committee, where he is a member of the Senate Arms Control Observer Group. He is also a member of the Congressional Friends of Ireland and a trustee of the John F. Kennedy Center for the Performing Arts in Washington, D.C.

Throughout his career, Kennedy has fought for issues that benefit the citizens of Massachusetts and the nation, including the effort to bring quality health care to every American, education reform, raising the minimum wage, defending the rights of workers and their families, strengthening the civil rights laws, assisting individuals with disabilities, fighting for cleaner water and cleaner air, and protecting and strengthening Social Security and Medicare for senior citizens.

Kennedy is the youngest of nine children of Joseph P. and Rose Fitzgerald Kennedy, and is a graduate of Harvard University and the University of Virginia Law School. His home is in Hyannis Port, Massachusetts, where he lives with his wife, Victoria Reggie Kennedy, and children, Curran and Caroline. He also has three grown children, Kara, Edward Jr., and Patrick, and four grandchildren.

Senior consulting editor STUART ANDERSON served as Executive Associate Commissioner for Policy and Planning and Counselor to the Commissioner at the Immigration and Naturalization Service from August 2001 until January 2003. He spent four and a half years on Capitol Hill on the Senate Immigration Subcommittee, first for Senator Spencer Abraham and then as Staff Director of the subcommittee for Senator Sam Brownback. Prior to that, he was Director of Trade and Immigration Studies at the Cato Institute in Washington, D.C., where he produced reports on the history of immigrants in the military and the role of immigrants in high technology. He currently serves as Executive Director of the National Foundation for American Policy, a nonpartisan public policy research organization focused on trade, immigration, and international relations. He has an M.A. from Georgetown University and a B.A. in Political Science from Drew University. His articles have appeared in such publications as the *Wall Street Journal*, *New York Times*, and *Los Angeles Times*.

MARIAN L. SMITH served as the senior historian of the U.S. Immigration and Naturalization Service (INS) from 1988 to 2003, and is currently the immigration and naturalization historian within the Department of Homeland Security in Washington, D.C. She studies, publishes, and speaks on the history of the immigration agency and is active in the management of official 20th-century immigration records.

PETER HAMMERSCHMIDT is the First Secretary (Financial and Military Affairs) for the Permanent Mission of Canada to the United Nations. Before taking this position, he was a ministerial speechwriter and policy specialist for the Department of National

CONTRIBUTORS

Defence in Ottawa. Prior to joining the public service, he served as the Publications Director for the Canadian Institute of Strategic Studies in Toronto. He has a B.A. (Honours) in Political Studies from Queen's University, and an MScEcon in Strategic Studies from the University of Wales, Aberystwyth. He currently lives in New York, where in his spare time he operates a freelance editing and writing service, Wordschmidt Communications.

Manuscript reviewer ESTHER OLAVARRIA serves as General Counsel to Senator Edward M. Kennedy, ranking Democrat on the U.S. Senate Judiciary Committee, Subcommittee on Immigration. She is Senator Kennedy's primary advisor on immigration, nationality, and refugee legislation and policies. Prior to her current job, she practiced immigration law in Miami, Florida, working at several nonprofit organizations. She cofounded the Florida Immigrant Advocacy Center and served as managing attorney, supervising the direct service work of the organization and assisting in the advocacy work. She also worked at Legal Services of Greater Miami, as the directing attorney of the American Immigration Lawyers Association Pro Bono Project, and at the Haitian Refugee Center, as a staff attorney. She clerked for a Florida state appellate court after graduating from the University of Florida Law School. She was born in Havana, Cuba, and raised in Florida.

Reviewer JANICE V. KAGUYUTAN is Senator Edward M. Kennedy's advisor on immigration, nationality, and refugee legislation and policies. Prior to working on Capitol Hill, Ms. Kaguyutan was a staff attorney at the NOW Legal Defense and Education Fund's Immigrant Women Program. Ms. Kaguyutan has written and trained extensively on the rights of immigrant victims of domestic violence, sexual assault, and human trafficking. Her previous work includes representing battered immigrant women in civil protection order, child support, divorce, and custody hearings, as well as representing immigrants before the Immigration and Naturalization Service on a variety of immigration matters.

NANCY HONOVICH attended New York University, where she received a B.A. in English and American Literature. She is the daughter of two Croatian immigrants.

PICTURE CREDITS

3m